Soirée Musicale

LANGUAGE OF DANCE SERIES

EDITOR	ASSOCIATE EDITOR
Ann Hutchinson Guest	**Ray Cook**
Director, Language of Dance Centre	Assistant Professor, Vassar College
London, UK	Poughkeepsie, New York, USA

No. 1:
The Flower Festival in Genzano: Pas de Deux
Edited by Ann Hutchinson Guest

No. 2:
Shawn's Fundamentals of Dance
Edited by Ann Hutchinson Guest

No. 3:
Nijinsky's *Faune* Restored
by Ann Hutchinson Guest
and Claudia Jeschke

No. 4:
Soirée Musicale
Edited by Ann Hutchinson Guest

Soirée Musicale

CHOREOGRAPHY BY

ANTONY TUDOR

SUITE OF MOVEMENTS FROM

GIOACHINO ROSSINI

ARRANGED BY BENJAMIN BRITTEN

NOTATED BY

ANN HUTCHINSON GUEST

THE NOVERRE PRESS

First published in 1993

This edition published in 2017 by
The Noverre Press
Southwold House
Isington Road
Binsted
Hampshire
GU34 4PH

Copyright © 2017 by Ann Hutchinson Guest.

ISBN 978-1-906830-79-3

Cover Photo: Maude Lloyd and Guy Massey dancing the *Canzonetta* in the January 1939 production.

Publication of the Labanotation score by kind permission of The Antony Tudor Ballet Trust, New York and of the Dance Notation Bureau, New York.
Cover photograph by Gordon Anthony. By courtesy of the Trustees of the Museum of The Theatre, a Branch of The Victoria and Albert Museum.
Photograph of Antony Tudor (page v) by Kenn Duncan.
Photograph of Peggy van Praagh (page x) by Gordon Anthony. Theatre Museum. Reproduced by courtesy of the Trustees of the Victoria and Albert Museum.
Photographs of Ann Hutchinson Guest rehearsing The Scottish Theatre Ballet (page 6) by Ian Cumming.
Photographs by Anthony Crickmay (pages 43, 51, 54, 64, 77 [top], 78 [top & bottom], 90 & 105 [bottom]). Theatre Museum. By courtesy of the Board of Trustees of The Victoria and Albert Museum.
Photographs of Rochelle Zide (pages 46 [bottom], 77 [bottom] & 78 [center]) by Will Rapport. Harvard Theatre Collection.
Photograph of London Ballet (page 46 [top]) by kind permission of Rambert Dance Company Archive.
Photograph of Ballet Rambert (page 105) from the collection of Michael Bayston.

All rights reserved. Permission for public performance must be obtained from The Dance Notation Bureau, 33 West 21 Street, New York, NY 10010, USA. No part of this book may be reproduced or utilized in any form or by any means, electronic or mechanical, including photocopying and recording, or by an information storage or retrieval system, without permission in writing from the publisher.

This book is lovingly dedicated to
Antony Tudor
in appreciation of his many rôles —
Tudor the Performer
Tudor the Choreographer
Tudor the Teacher
Tudor the Inspirer
Tudor of Sharp, Witty Tongue
Tudor the Believer in the Rôle of Labanotation in Dance Education
Tudor Himself, a Rare Human Being

(Kenn Duncan)

CONTENTS

Introduction to the Series ix

Foreword xi

Acknowledgements xiii

Historical Background 1

Casting 3

Costumes 4

Study and Performance Notes 7

Labanotation Glossary 36

The Choreographic Score of *Soirée Musicale* 41
    Opening March 42
    Canzonetta 54
    Tirolese 64
    Bolero 77
    Neapolitan 87
    Finale 94

Appendix - Notes on the Music 106

INTRODUCTION TO THE SERIES

The *Language of Dance Series* aims to expand the literature of dance through publication of key works that cover a range of dance styles and dance periods.

A language is spoken, written and read. Those intimately involved in the study and performance of dance will have experienced the language of dance in its "spoken" form, i.e., when it is danced. During the years spent in mastering dance, the component parts are discovered and become part of one's dance language. Through its written form these component parts, the 'building blocks' common to all forms of dance, become clear, as well as how these blocks are used. The study of the Language of Dance incorporates these basic elements and the way they are put together to produce choreographic sentences. How the movement sequences are performed, the manner of "uttering" them, rests on the individual's interpretation.

Through careful selection of appropriate movement description, these gems of dance heritage have been translated into Labanotation, the highly developed method of analyzing and recording movement.

In the *Language of Dance Series* understanding of the material is enriched through study and performance notes which provide an aid in exploring the movement sequences and bringing the choreography to life. Whenever possible there is included historical background to place the work in context, and additional information of value to researchers and dance scholars.

Dr. Ann Hutchinson Guest, Editor

Peggy van Praagh, the leading dancer in the Bolero when *Soirée Musicale* was originally performed in 1938 and again when it was produced by the London Ballet in January 1940.

(Gordon Anthony)

FOREWORD

How fortunate I was that my dancing career coincided with that of Antony Tudor. Those years between 1930 and 1940 when Marie Rambert was passionately and patiently nurturing us were packed with creativity and innovation.

Frederick Ashton was already pouring out little gems of ballets and Andreé Howard was producing her delicate and evocative works when Antony tried out his first choreographic movement — on me, as it happened. We were standing in the wings waiting for a rehearsal to begin. That was in 1931, and the ballet he had in mind was to be *Crossgartered,* from Shakespeare's *Twelfth Night*. I think I realized even then that he was breaking new ground, searching to find movements which could convey real emotions, while using the classical idiom.

There are very few of Tudor's works that one could call abstract, or pure dance. *Soirée Musicale* is one of them. He choreographed it to be an opening ballet when he formed his own company The London Ballet. It is a gentle, happy ballet with no psychological undertones, and with ravishing costumes by Hugh Stevenson. *Gala Performance* which he made soon after may have seemed in the same vein, but was based strongly on the characters and temperaments of the three ballerinas, French, Russian and Italian.

Antony's choice of music reflected and echoed his search to express deep human emotions held firmly within the bounds of classical ballet. Working with him was for me a constant exploration, exciting, challenging and fulfilling.

Maude Lloyd Gosling

ACKNOWLEDGEMENTS

To start at the beginning, I must first thank the late Dame Peggy van Praagh for inviting me to notate *Soirée Musicale* at the time she was teaching it to the Rambert Company, and also the late Dame Marie Rambert for allowing the intrusion which included briefly following the company on tour to get the final details. It was Antony Tudor's belief in notation that encouraged me to obtain his permission to publish the score. Since then Sally Brayley Bliss, Trustee of the Antony Tudor Ballet Trust, has given assistance in the completion of details. Thanks also to the Antony Tudor Ballet Trust for a generous donation which made possible the inclusion of so many photographs.

For comments on the Study and Performance Notes I turned to dancers who had performed the work. Rochelle Zide had danced in it in the USA and had worked with Tudor, checking my original score. Her suggestions and highlightings were most valuable. John O'Brien and Michael Bayston, both Rambert dancers, gave encouragement and reassurance as well as additional thoughts.

Photographs were not easy to come by; *Soirée* is one of Tudor's less well-known ballets and hence did not receive the attention that was given to *Lilac Garden*, *Dark Elegies*, *Pillar of Fire,* or other of his ground-breaking ballets. I am grateful to Rochelle Zide, Michael Bayston and Sarah Woodcock at the Theatre Museum for their help in locating relevant and illuminating photographs.

In finalizing the Labanotation score I acknowledge with appreciation the contributions of Muriel Topaz, Airi Hynninen and Rochelle Zide in incorporating adjustments made by Tudor himself.

I am indebted to the following in assisting my research into the ballet and its many performances: Jane Pritchard at the Rambert Archives; Edward Pask, archivist at the Australian Ballet; Harry Haythorne, director of the New Zealand Ballet; Elizabeth Watson of the Scottish Theatre Archive at Glasgow University Library; Christina Kaut, archivist at the National Ballet of Canada; Denise Collett-Simpson at the Royal Academy of Dancing library; and Mary Clarke at the *Dancing Times*. Peter Brinson gave helpful information, as did Maude Lloyd Gosling, who also contributed the foreword.

The autography for the Labanotation score was prepared by Irene Politis and Maggie Burke Lewis, to whom I am indebted for their painstaking work. Ray Cook has been an invaluable associate editor with his precise and critical eye for accuracy and consistency throughout the book. Clarity in the wording has been assured through Juli Nunlist's generous painstaking checking of the text. Coordination of the project and production of the book have been in the capable hands of Jane Dulieu. Always helpful in unearthing pertinent books and facts is my husband Ivor Guest who finds moments to be helpful in between his own research and writing; the time he spared is much appreciated.

HISTORICAL BACKGROUND

Although he did not mould the style of a great international company, as did Balanchine and Ashton, and although he generally worked within a frame of modest dimensions, Antony Tudor (1909-1987) is today recognised as one of the most innovative and influential choreographers of the twentieth century. A mature pupil of Marie Rambert, he chose to follow the creative line rather than that of the performer. Working on a small scale as the straitened finances of the time dictated, he revealed a rare gift for expressing psychological insight in the dance. Thereby he greatly expanded ballet's horizons, adding a new dimension to its potential as drama. His *Lilac Garden* and *Dark Elegies*, which he produced for Ballet Rambert in the late 1930s, were major masterpieces of this genre which were touched by a subtle depth of feeling never before captured in dance theatre.

Soirée Musicale, which dates from the same period, is a lighter work, a *divertissement* of ineffable charm set to Benjamin Britten's suite based on pieces by Rossini. Britten had originally written this suite, scored for a small orchestra and voices - his opus 9, and entitled *Soirées Musicales* (in the plural) - for a short film publicising the Post Office savings Bank. It was too good to be cast aside, and when Tudor showed interest in it, Britten revised it for a larger orchestra and omitted the choral part. The suite was in four movements, and legend has it that in conceiving his choreography, Tudor had in mind four of the great ballerinas of the Romantic period, Lucile Grahn for the *Canzonetta*, Marie Taglioni for the *Tirolese*, Fanny Elssler for the *Bolero* and Fanny Cerrito for the *Tarantella*. It may not be entirely coincidental that the year in which Tudor's ballet was first performed also saw the publication of Beaumont and Sitwell's superb volume of reproductions of Romantic ballet lithographs.

Tudor's choice of designer was Hugh Stevenson (1910-56), another Rambert *protégée*, who had designed several of Tudor's early ballets for Ballet Rambert, including *Lilac Garden,* and was working on several commissions for The London Ballet which Tudor formed in 1938 after leaving Rambert.

Soirée Musicale was first performed at a Cecchetti Society *matinée* at the Palladium Theatre, London, on November 26th, 1938, the leading parts being danced by Gerd Larsen and Hugh Laing *(Canzonetta)*, Maude Lloyd and Antony Tudor *(Tirolese)*, Peggy van Praagh *(Bolero)*, and Monica Boam and Guy Massey *(Tarantella)*. A few weeks later, on December 12th, 1938, it entered the repertory of The London Ballet during its short season at Toynbee Hall. The London Ballet had a brief existence, but as Tudor's platform during the brief period before he went to America to join the newly-formed Ballet Theatre, it made a considerable contribution to the nascent English ballet.

In an early review of *Soirée Musicale* in **The Dancing Times** (June 1939) "The Sitter Out" commented on the variety in the four movements - *"the gay Tirolese...brimful of spirit, the Bolero...fascinatingly Spanish in feeling, and the Tarantella...lightly Italian"* - and praised Tudor for having *"gained all this atmosphere by suggestion and not by a forcing of authentic national steps"*.

On the merger of The London Ballet with the Ballet Rambert in June 1940, *Soirée Musicale* entered the Rambert repertory. The Labanotation score was prepared in the Spring of 1962 when Peggy van Praagh produced a revival of the work for Ballet Rambert.

The ballet has also been revived by Peggy van Praagh for the Robert Joffrey Ballet in 1959. The first reconstruction of the ballet from the Labanotation score was by Rochelle Zide in the USA, a production which was checked by Antony Tudor. Later Tudor gave permission for Ann Hutchinson to revive the ballet for Scottish Theatre Ballet in 1972, for the Royal New Zealand Ballet in 1985, for the Rambert school in 1986, and for the Central Ballet School in 1987.

Ivor Guest

The set by Hugh Stevenson depicts a gracious salon, with pillars,
a high arch, chandelier and two elegant chaises longues upstage
at either side - a charming setting for an evening of dance.

CASTING

All the dances in this ballet are elegant. The three *pas de deux*, the Canzonetta, Tirolese and Tarantella (Neapolitan) must be danced by three pairs who are good partners and take pleasure in dancing with each other. The Tirolese and Tarantella (Neapolitan) are quick, light-hearted classical versions of national dances, lightly showing off the dancers' prowess. Of the three men and six women the following strengths are required:

Canzonetta: This is a romantic duo with its own lyrical quality. The woman should have good balance and be able to sustain flowing movements. She must have some gift of mime: the stylized gestures have an inner meaning which should not be lost. She should preferably be young: the *pas de deux* comes across well as a tentative relationship between two somewhat shy young people. The man must be good at lifts, particularly for those in which he carries the girl across stage in a *grand jeté en avant* position. He also needs to imbue the movements with meaning and know how to carry himself and sustain the performance element while merely walking across stage. He should be an ardent young 'princely' type, with good feeling for 'line'.

Tirolese: This bright, light-hearted dance is not technically difficult, but shading in the performance of the steps and well-placed emphasis (or lack of it) makes the dance more than just another Tirolese. The piece is well suited to small dancers who are fleet of foot. There is only one lift for which timing and momentum are needed more than strength. Musicality is important because of *ritardandos* in the music. A feeling for character dance is also important - a weightedness with rebound.

Bolero: This dance for three women is demanding: it requires great stage presence and a commanding focus on the audience, as well as stylized movement which is 'shot through' with wry humour. The expression of several movements is definitely tongue-in-cheek, almost a teasing of the audience, but done (apparently) in all seriousness. In the Bolero there is a certain formality; the carriage of the head and the hypnotic *misterioso* expression in the eyes are important, especially when the dancers are facing the audience. The three women must be strong on *pointe*; this is particularly true for the leading dancer. The emphasis in this dance is more on rhythmic security than on the sense of tempo change featured in the Tirolese and that of phrasing in the Canzonetta.

Tarantella: For this variation both dancers must have speed so that the swift steps are
(Neapolitan) performed neatly and accurately. The woman needs swift *pirouettes* and clean *entrechat sixes*. The man needs strong double *tours* and *sixes*; indeed, of the three male dancers he should be technically the strongest. As a couple they should be particularly vivacious since their dance leads into the whole Finale of the ballet. There are a few lifts in the Finale, in particular the man must be strong enough to hold the woman by the waist over his head for a few beats.

All the dancers must have a sense of social give-and-take, how to lead their partners back to the chaises longues, to acknowledge other people and, while others are dancing, to be alive and interested without catching the eye of the audience through too much action. They must also stay in character. It is all a question of that elusive quality: style.

Identification	Original Cast* (1938)
C = Canzonetta Woman	C = Gerd Larsen
MC = Her Partner	MC = Hugh Laing
T = Tirolese Woman	T = Maude Lloyd
MT = Her Partner	MT = Antony Tudor
B1 = Leading Bolero Woman	B1 = Peggy van Praagh
B2 = Her Companion	B2 = Charlotte Bidmead
B3 = Her Companion	B3 = Rosa Vernon
N = Neapolitan (Tarantella) Woman	N = Monica Boam
MN = Her Partner	MN = Guy Massey

From Dance Perspectives No. 18 *Antony Tudor. Part Two: The Years in America and After.* Selma Jeanne Cohen.

COSTUMES

Hugh Stevenson (1910-1946) was one of the most successful of British designers for ballet having created designs not only for several of Tudor's ballets (including *Soirée Musicale*) but also for Ninette de Valois, Andree Howard and John Cranko.

Canzonetta

The costume is white with a pale bluish tinge.

Black jacket with white shirt and tights, a pale blue sash and detail on the collar.

COSTUMES

Tirolese

A rose-colored apron and bodice, the bodice being striped black. The skirt has a pinkish hue.

A plum-colored shirt is featured here. The green hat is not usually worn.

Bolero

Lavender-pink underskirt and bodice with a swathing of black lace draped around the white skirt.

White skirt, bodice with black stripes, and black lace draped around the skirt.

Neapolitan
(Tarantella)

Orange, yellow, green and black scarves adorn the skirt and are also used for the headdress.

Reddish-brown details on the jacket are featured. The hat is not usually worn.

Ann Hutchinson Guest rehearsing The Scottish Theatre Ballet, November 1972.

Floor plans were handed out to each of the dancers. Here they are being explained to Michael Beare and Hilary Debden.

Getting the feel of a moment in the Bolero with Ann Hutchinson Guest demonstrating in the foreground, dancers left to right are: Amanda Olivier, Patricia Rianne, Sally Collard-Gentle.

STUDY AND PERFORMANCE NOTES

As the title suggests, the scene is an elegant drawing room in which two chaises longues are placed across the upstage corners. Six ladies and three gentlemen are gathered for a musical evening, dancing together for their own enjoyment, an enjoyment which is transmitted to the audience.

There is no story line as such. In each of the *pas de deux* there is a clear relationship between the lady and the gentleman. Except for the Canzonetta, in which the pair are much engrossed with each other, the dancers invite the audience into their world at specific moments when their full focus is on the audience. After a lively start the piece moves through changes in pace and energy, culminating in the Neapolitan (Tarantella) which leads directly into the Finale. This ending, though bursting with energy, is still performed in an elegant manner.

In the following notes measure numbers are indicated in square brackets, thus: [23].

General Notes

Depending on the size of stage and energy of the dancers, there are moments when adjustments need to be made in traveling to achieve the spatial patterns on the floor plans. A little 'cheating' is sometimes needed (e.g., the crossing patterns of the Opening March [57-64] for the partners and those of [65-72] for the women). Some may need to take larger or smaller steps than written. Traveling at slightly more or less of an angle is not spelled out in the notation but is indicated in the floor plans; an example is the zig-zagging traveling in the Tirolese during [22-26]. Identification of the floor plans does not indicate the exact count when traveling starts or ends; this is clearly stated in the movement score.

Throughout the ballet there are key moments when partners should look at each other. Such focus is not to be maintained in a rigid way, but should 'dissolve' naturally according to the movement and individual expression of the dancers, i.e., there is some leeway regarding the duration of such statement of looking. However, at key moments when looking at the partner should occur, the statement is repeated. In a ballet of this kind personal interpretation on the part of the performers includes freedom in choosing appropriate minor variations in head movements; these will vary from dancer to dancer and therefore should not be indicated as part of the choreography.

For those becoming familiar with the score and following it while the music is playing, a device for repeated phrases is used, giving the outline of the footwork for the eye to follow; accompanying repeat signs in brackets placed on the left indicate that the material is an exact repetition of the earlier phrase and all details of arms, head, etc., should be applied.

Opening March

The opening march contains an *intrada* leading into a promenade around the room. Note the coordination in this section between music and dance: for the dance, the 2/4 metre is usually counted in sequences of 2 or 4 measures. There is a 10-count sequence near the beginning. Where it is helpful for the dancers, counts are given according to the phrasing of the music, these are indicated as dancer's counts (see **Labanotation Glossary, p. 34**). They are quite logical and are based on the regular music beat. To facilitate reading, bar lines are drawn in the dance score only for every second measure.

The ladies are arranged around the stage in poses which reflect some of what is to come. They are waiting for the gentlemen to arrive and begin the 'festivities'. Three women, N, B2, B3, near the wings, face outward towards the corners where the men will enter. The center three women, C, T and B1, are arranged in the pose of the souvenir Romantic ballet lithograph of the Three Graces. They are three of the four women who have leading rôles.

Intrada

In the opening section the choreography expresses young people enjoying one another's company. The initial bow, taking of hands, and preliminary movements leading up to the promenade serve as an 'introduction', with the promenade itself and the steps that conclude it as a 'conversation piece'. At such a social gathering, with only three men, it is inevitable that a change of partners takes place, and that the introductions and 'getting-to-know-you' are repeated. What dance material has Tudor used? The ordinary events described above are couched in stylized forms which are realised through crafting classical ballet technique to achieve each special effect. The set and costumes provide the sense of elegance needed, a basic dignity underlying the vivacity.

The opening two measures of the music establish the tempo of the March, and provide the introduction needed by the dancers. During the *intrada* and promenade the outer couples move identically; the 'Three Graces' in the center remain still

[3-9] The men enter immediately[1] facing their partners and greet them with a dry elegant bow, the right arm sweeping from out to the side, across via forward, so that the hand ends near the left shoulder. Each immediately proffers his right hand to his partner who, stepping in toward him with a forward *piqué* [2] and, taking hands across, performs a half-swivel turn under his arm. She then reverses the turn so that she ends facing him again. These swivel turns are crisp with a pause at the end of each. Each woman then steps back and, releasing hands, the partners perform a *port de bras* from forward out to the side to form a large oval circle with rounded arms, elbows lifted (an exaggerated elbow rotation) and hands almost touching (counts 7-10). Both bend their torsos forward as the arms open, the women turning their heads to the left, the men to the right, each thus looking into the same direction. Note that the counts given here

---

[1] In practice they are often already on stage.

[2] Glossary: *piqué* or *posé* step - a quick step onto *pointe* for the woman, half-toe for the man.

encompass the music phrase, which contains an extra measure of two beats.

Transition to Promenade

[10-11] Next comes a 4-count transition into a promenade around the room. Facing into the clockwise direction of this circle, each woman takes three small steps and a slight spring backward onto both feet. Meanwhile each man circles around his partner with long steps arriving at her right side. Depending on the size of the stage the couples may need to back up as much as possible during these four counts so that more distance is available for the promenade around the room.

Promenade

[12-27] Holding both hands, right to right, left to left and looking at each other, the couples proceed clockwise around the room with a bright, jaunty air, expressed by the quick 'catch step' in what would otherwise be a straight forward walk. On count 4 of the 8-count phrase both take a forward *piqué* step, but, almost teasingly, while the woman takes the free left leg forward into a front *attitude*, the man takes his leg backward into an *arabesque*. The repeat of the 'catch step' leads into a low step followed by a *relevé* (rise) with the woman now in *arabesque*, the man in a front *attitude*. Releasing left hands, they both perform a *piqué-ballonné* step, the man traveling across in front of the woman to face the opposite direction. Two quick steps on the spot for both precede a low forward step into *arabesque* so that their left shoulders are now almost touching, their right arms overhead. These two measures are more 'intimate' in contrast to the formality of the promenading. Before repeating the promenade, the woman walks a small circular pattern to the left (without change of front) while the man walks around her to end at her right side again. During this transition they should try to move backward in the line of the circle. They take hands as before for the repeat of the 8-count phrase of the promenade, which concludes, as before, with the *ballonné* phrase of eight counts. During this phrase the couples look at each other, in a natural, 'free' way.

[28-29] Having turned her back to the center of the circle, each woman moves toward the corner of the stage nearest her by taking a long, sliding, forward *chassé* step into a *relevé* in *attitude*, while her partner steps backward into a *soutenu* turn to the left; both take the arms up into fifth position.

[30-35] As the man kneels back, now facing out from the circle, his partner takes a *coupé* under step on *pointe* and turns left ending with her left shoulder in toward the center of the circle as she lowers into a fourth position lunge, leaning in toward her partner. The size and exact direction of the steps here may need to be adjusted: the partners must be close enough so the man's right hand can take her left as she performs a half-circle around him with a quick 'limping' step, the weight partially taken forward on *pointe* before the back leg *coupés* under. A little unfolding of her leg before each partial step provides dainty articulation. As she circles, the woman's right hand holds the side-middle part of her skirt and brings it up to her hip. After this 'token' circling of her partner (actually less than a half-circle), she heads toward center stage to take the place of one of the 'Three Graces', who, having held still up to this point, now come into action.

N, B2, B3

[36-43] As the erstwhile outer women move into the center, they repeat the long *chassé* and *relevé* into *attitude* phrase, now performed facing center stage (the center of their circle). This is followed by the same 'limping' step, now performed with the three women circling clockwise following each other.

C, B1, T (and partners)

[44-48] In this next phrase the couples perform a modified version of the opening phrase which led into the promenade. The man offers his right hand to his partner, who takes it with her right; they take left hands also, and the woman does a crisp *piqué* turn under his arms, pausing a moment before she steps back away from him to perform, as before, the *port de bras* into the oval-shaped arm design; their heads looking into the clockwise direction of the circle, the direction in which, in a moment, they will be promenading. The previous preparatory 'backing up' steps used to get into position are now cut short to only two counts into position onstage.

C, B1, T (and partners)

[49-56] The promenade phrase now repeats, as before, but the 4-count walk around at the end is modified to place all three couples facing front; two are now located in the front corner areas of the stage, the third couple, T and MN being center back.

C, B2, T

[36-43] These women who were previously in the center move out to the men to become their new partners. To cover enough space as they move away from center they may have to take one or two steps before the long *chassé* into *relevé* in *attitude*. As they *chassé* the men rise performing a *soutenu* turn to the left (adjusting spacing if need be) and finish once more on the left knee. As happened with the previous women, they circle their partners with the 'limping' step, performing a full circle around them.

N, B2, B3

[44-48] During this transition phrase, N, B2, B3, now in the center take a long *chassé* into *attitude*, facing in, each one with her hands under the elbows of her neighbors. This contact helps balance, as the dancers stay on *pointe* for four counts. They come down with a *coupé* into *pointe tendue* forward.

N, B2, B3

[49-56] During this second promenade the center women travel counterclockwise with their left arms up, hands touching (as in a 'star' formation). They perform three *piqué-coupé* steps before turning to perform three on the other side, circling clockwise, now with right arms up, hands touching.

C, B1, T (and partners)

[57-64] The second promenade concluded, the couples start a crossing and separating pattern, each man and woman crossing with a *coupé-ballonné-sauté-posé-jeté croisé en avant* sequence, and then, alternating sides, crossing each other, twice more, the path being a shallow zig-zag, traveling slightly downstage. Although they are not looking directly at each other there is an awareness, a relating while they are moving toward and away. Note that to cover space in the zig-zag crossing, the dancers will need to travel also on each *coupé-ballonné-sauté* so that the floor pattern is clear. This extra traveling is not spelled out in the notation. The crossing concludes with the woman stepping in to her partner with a 'lame duck' *piqué* turn (an *en dehors piqué* turn). Her partner steps toward her, arms open, and the phrase ends with her placing one hand on his arm for balance.

N, B2, B3

[57-64] During the zig-zag step these center women circle counterclockwise with a gentle forward traveling 'limping' step, chests facing the center of the circle; their arms are linked, each hand grasping the elbow of a neighbor. On the eighth step each turns inward and retraces her path with the same steps on the other side. Their concern is only with each other.

The quick transition at the end of [64], which leads into the next phrase is spelled out for each of the men and for the three women, B1, T, C.

Women

[65-72] A different kind of crossing now takes place. The six women cross each other back to back in pairs, the transition at the end of [64] having been a preparation for this move. The women's sideward *dos à dos* crossing step [65-70] requires stepping out and some spatial adjustment to make both their relationship and the path clear. After the third crossing, an adjusting traveling '*chassé*' step into a 'lame duck' *piqué* turn carries each into the appropriate direction and place for the next phrase. For B1, C and T the destination is for each to arrive in front of her partner who places his hands on her waist. N and B2 end downstage near the front corners, while B3 ends center upstage.

Men

[65-72] At the start of the section the men 'get out of the way', so to speak, with a traveling *assemblé en tournant* toward center stage, arriving in a triangular formation, MC in front. On [63] they wait, left hand on hip.

Women

[73-80] An accumulating pattern evolves next. The two downstage women, N and B2, cross on a curved path, starting with a preparatory *chassé-coupé-chassé* step into an *en dehors piqué* turn, both covering as much ground as possible. The turn features a *développé* with full *port de bras* (arms moving from *bras bas* through 1st, 5th and 2nd positions), the body inclining away and then toward the unfolding leg which ends with a *tombé* leading into a repeat of the phrase. On the repeat B1, C and T join in along the curved paths already established. On the third time B3 joins in, but by now the final destination, the end of this section, must be anticipated and the degree of travel and stage location adjusted accordingly.

Men

[73-80] They continue to wait [73-78], left hand on hip, except for a moment of supporting a woman, until the end of this section [79, 80].

All the dancers end facing the audience.

Transition to Canzonetta

[79-80] As a transition into the first *pas de deux*, the phrase ends with all running to their places on or behind the chaises except C and MC, who run to the downstage right corner to be ready to start their *pas de deux*. With the other women all sitting on the chaises and the other men standing behind them, the scene is set for the Canzonetta.

Canzonetta

This *pas de deux* is youthful and lyrical, allowing scope for charm and moments of intimacy. It has a light, gentle, sometimes slightly subdued 'flavor', yet it is also outgoing. For the most part the two dancers are concerned only with each other.

[1-2] The starting pose in the downstage right corner, facing downstage right, has them holding right hands, with the man's left arm around the woman's waist. The couple begins by traveling swiftly backward, and, releasing right hands, each performs a full outward *port de bras* with the right arm. The woman follows her right hand with her gaze as it circles. The man looks only at her. They travel as far back on the diagonal as possible to give maximum distance for the next step.

[3-4] On the first dance phrase they move forward on the same room diagonal, but now with a flirtatious sequence. In unison they step forward with the right foot into a *jeté* with both legs in low *attitude derrière*. The woman circles both arms on a parallel path to the right, up and

over to the left, her body bending right and then left, augmenting the arm circle and helping to achieve more lift in the *jeté*. The man uses only his right arm, as his left hand remains at the left side of the woman's waist. The tempo here is a little slow for what would normally be a high *allegro* spring; thus lift on the take-off and cushioning on the landing are needed to make the *jeté* more '*adagio*'. After landing on the left foot from the *jeté* both rise on that foot, a moment of uplift overcurve into the low step that follows. For the woman this low step is the preparation for a *piqué* forward on *pointe* with the left foot, a *piqué* which is held while she performs little *ronds de jambe* with the right leg in front *attitude*. This movement (known as *jouer* in the Cecchetti method) is performed with the hands held near the working foot, the body (chest) leaning well forward over that leg. The man has both hands on her waist and, with a long lunge forward on his right leg just past her right side, he helps her balance, looking up at her. At the end of the *jouer* he steps across to her left side (still slightly behind her) and again looks up at her. Just as he takes his new position she steps forward on *pointe* into a front *attitude* with her left leg. Leaning away from him and unfolding her left arm sideward above his head, she looks at him under this arm. Her right arm is bent in front of her body, though not especially close. This hand position suggests coyness, a little of which is appropriate, but only a little, for it can too easily be overdone.

[5-8] To repeat this whole first dance phrase, the man must step enough to his right to reach the woman's right side again. The *jeté* and *jouer* phrases are performed twice more. The woman concludes the phrase with a step forward toward downstage right. If they have traveled too far into the corner her spacing can be adjusted at the start of the next phrase with a couple of unobtrusive 'backing up' steps performed when the focus is on the man.

[9-12] The man now walks on a slightly curved path to the other side of the stage, the exact number of steps for this walk being left open. The traveling should have flow and some unevenness, that is, not be totally predictable; it should give the impression that he is letting the movement take over as it responds to the music and his mood. On arrival he makes a gracious gesture to the woman as though saying, "I give this moment to you". She responds with a *croisé* step toward him in preparation for a *grand renversé* (a full *grand rond de jambe en tournant*) with her right leg, her right arm opening out with the leg and circling upward as the left arm circles downward, the two meeting in 1st while her working leg lowers into fifth to continue the turn on both feet. She ends with a *croisé* step toward downstage right, arms open as she watches her partner. Just as she concludes this phrase he responds with the same, performing the *rond de jambe* on the other side. His concluding turn blends into swift traveling to return to his partner, whom he reaches just in time for the lift that follows.

[13-14] The woman prepares with a step backward to get close to her partner before rising into a *grand jeté en avant*, the man lifting her and turning her to face the direction of travel (to stage left). She must look as though she is performing an extended *grand jeté* as he carries her across the front of the stage. A static carrying in *grand jeté* position must be avoided. The lift may appear to be unexpected, and she may reflect surprise and pleasure. He places her down in *arabesque alongée*; then, both facing front, they perform a *jeté à côté* to the right into a full *soutenu* turn with full *port de bras*.

[15-18] These larger movements are now followed by a quiet passage in which, facing downstage right and holding inside hands, they travel backward stepping on the right foot into

a low *cabriole en arrière* followed by a linking step to repeat this *cabriole*. On the first *cabriole* they look away from each other (a shyness or uncertain about a moment of intimacy?), but they look at each other on the sustained forward *chassé* step on the left foot which leads into a *pas de chat*. This *pas de chat*, which takes the place of the previous *jeté à côté*, leads into a repeat of the *soutenu* turn, the arms again making a full *port de bras*. As before, this leads into the backward *cabriole* pattern. But this time the man looks at his partner from the start; her gaze goes to him on the second *cabriole*. On this repeat the slower *chassé* forward on the left foot is even more marked, it results in the center of weight leading into a 'run'[3] forward into the next flirtatious phrase, the woman looking back at her partner over her left shoulder during her run.

[19-20] The 'run' leads to a *piqué* into *arabesque* on which the woman's hands are near her mouth. Sustaining the *arabesque*, with her left hand she makes a gesture suggestive of blowing a kiss, the arm unfolding softly forward high while the right arm unfolds to the side. As her arms extend, she again looks backward to the man over her left shoulder. Since the 'kiss' is not blown toward him, it is as though she is teasing him. This action of 'blowing a kiss' should not be too literally performed; a suggestion of it is more in keeping with the style of the dance. A low step on the left foot coming off the *piqué* leads into two quick preparatory steps (a rudimentary open *glissade en avant*) into a repeat of the *piqué arabesque*, with her hands again near her mouth to blow a second 'kiss'. While she thus travels away from him, the man stands still, watching her, his left hand near his heart. This gesture also needs to be suggested rather than spelled out.

[21-22] Having traveled away from the man the woman now moves toward him, taking a *piqué* turn in *attitude* to face him and then a low forward step followed by a quick sketchy *glissade* as a preparation for a *piqué* into a high *attitude devant*, at which point she places her right hand in the man's right hand. He also starts the phrase with an *attitude* turn, but to the left, ending on a *fondu* facing her before he takes the same rudimentary open '*glissade*' steps, but traveling backward as she advances toward him. As she takes her front *attitude piqué*, he takes a low backward step into a front *attitude*. He offers her his right hand for her to take; both have their arms in an *arabesque* line. After a transition step, each repeats the front *attitude*. These steps have carried them toward upstage left.

[23-24] Now they turn into profile, the woman facing stage left, the man stage right. Still holding hands, left shoulder to left shoulder, they raise their right arms up and step toward stage left (the man stepping backward) into an *arabesque fondue*, each with the left arm sweeping downward between them to a long forward *arabesque* line. Sustaining that position for a moment, they step again toward stage left and then, with the two quick '*glissade*-like' steps, return to the stage diagonal line and repeat the *piqué* in front *attitude* pattern as before.

[25-30] Having released hands in [24], the man faces front, his arms in second position, while the woman takes a *piqué* forward to stage left and, with full *port de bras*, raises her left leg forward and then with a slow *fouetté* turns into *arabesque* facing stage right. At this point the

---

[3] The word 'run' is used for swift, light traveling steps with heels off the ground, not for a run in the sense of leaving the floor between steps.

music swells in volume supporting the choreographic development in which the larger movement and close proximity of the dancers provide an inner intensity and a new dimension to their relationship. On this slow *fouetté* turn the woman balances by herself as long as possible, the man catching her waist when need be, certainly at the start of the slow *penché* which follows. During this *penché* the woman carries her right arm down and then 'backward' near her body, the gesture being toward the man as she turns her shoulders and head slightly to the left as though looking back at him. In fact she cannot see him, but the audience gets the impression of a look toward him. Sweeping her right arm down again and then up to a high *arabesque* line, she comes upright. Perhaps as though this intimacy is too much, she runs to the downstage left corner and stands looking back at the man over her right shoulder. As she departs he picks up the cue and runs to the downstage right corner. Perhaps to reassure her, he then repeats the *grand renversé* step which she had introduced and he had echoed earlier [10-12]. She again echoes this phrase, as he did before, and ends looking at her partner.

[31-35] There is a moment's pause, then the man walks across to downstage left on a curved path, his exact path and steps being according to his response to the music and to this moment in the dance. He arrives just in time to pick her up for a repeat on the other side of the *grand jeté en avant* lift across the front of the stage. As he sets her down onto her right foot they both perform a step-hop-hop traveling forward in an *arabesque alongé*, toward stage right, arms in third *arabesque*. The man may leave his left arm around the woman's waist; otherwise they move identically at this point. The hops are followed by a *croisé* undercurve *chassé* step to downstage right, the arms opening in second. The lift and hopping steps (the two-measure phrase) are then repeated to the other side traveling to stage left.

[36-39] A diagonal crossing of heightened intensity now occurs. The dancers start facing front as they take a swift suspended diagonal *piqué* step away from each other, the body leaning toward the partner, arms in 3rd, away from the partner. This step has the feeling of an intake of breath before something important is said. Three traveling steps lead into a *grand assemblé battu porté*, the arms rising swiftly up in fifth to express (and provide) greater uplift. Having exchanged places there is a slight pause before they take a rather deliberate *chassé* step toward each other into a *relevé* in *attitude*. During the *chassé* the arm follows a path forward before opening out to the side into the usual *attitude* arm position. This face-to-face pose is sustained for a moment before they repeat the diagonal step away from each other (again facing front) and also the crossing steps ending with the same *grand assemblé*. However, this time there is no pause after landing from the *assemblé*, instead an immediate rebound into the *relevé* occurs, the appropriate arm moving at once sideward to the *attitude* position. This position is again suspended before a transition into the next section. The man takes a few steps moving further toward center stage, the woman 'runs' toward him and the just-completed bright, lively, full-blooded sequence of [36-39] changes to a few moments of sustained *adagio*.

[40-43] Arriving close to her partner the woman takes a *piqué* onto her right foot by his right side. With the man supporting her waist she raises her left leg forward, her arms rising to fifth. Slowly she turns to the right into *arabesque*, the man adjusting his hold. Facing downstage left, arms still overhead, she gradually twists her upper body to the right and bends diagonally backward, curving around the man in a very stylized 'caress'. A gradual recovery leads into a 'run' to the downstage left corner, her arms lowering as she goes. She ends *croisé* with head and arms directed toward her partner.

[43-46] After watching her go, the man runs toward her into a low lunge in which he leans to his right, his arms extended sideward, the left high, the right low, palms 'down'. It is as though he is calling for her attention, establishing that he is going to 'say something'. With his right arm he gestures toward her with an undercurve path led by the inside of his lower arm, his hand passing near her right shoulder. This gesture leads to a rise in *attitude* with the arm 'gathering' into the Eros *attitude* arm position. Having thus 'caught her full attention', he turns and takes several steps past center stage into a flamboyant *fouetté sauté battu*, both arms up. On coming down on his left foot he lowers onto his right knee (a fourth position foot-kneel) as he carries his right arm 'backward' and downward into a heartfelt gesture forward toward his partner. This gesture includes the body and the forward pull has the effect of pulling him forward into a run to her ending at her left side. The timing of this 'solo' can be left to the dancer, but it must relate appropriately to the music.

[47-51] Now side by side, the man at the left with his right hand on the woman's waist, they both perform the same large *port de bras* as that at the start of their duet [1-2], but this time remaining on the spot and using the left arm. As before this *port de bras* leads to the *jeté* in low *attitude derrière*, but this time the step into it and the traveling is backward. Then with the man's left hand at her waist, the woman takes a *piqué* backward into a front *attitude* to perform the *jouer ronds de jambe*, as before, but now with her left leg. The man again watches her, first at her left side and then on her right as she changes weight into a front *attitude* on the left foot, her right arm unfolding, as before, over his head as she looks under it at him, her left hand in a light, delicate position in front of her chest. This phrase is then repeated (again backward). It should be noted that this sagittal transposition of [3 and 4] from forward to backward is physically more difficult than one might expect, and for a smooth performance requires much practice.

[52-59] The concluding sequence of the dance which follows usually requires considerable practice. Achievement of the correct relationships depends largely on the heights and length of limb of the performers. Where some can master the positions and transitions with ease, others experience difficulty. Starting facing downstage left, away from the man, the woman steps forward into a half-turn *relevé* to the left, the free foot in a low *retiré*. As she steps and rises, her left arm unfolds upward. The man catches her around the waist as she does a slow *développé* forward with her right leg past the right side of his body. She then bends slowly backward and gradually recovers, bringing her free leg down and then into *retiré* as she swivels a half-turn to the right. As she turns she unfolds her right arm upward to join the left before both arms lower to come to rest, her right hand on his right shoulder, her left on his left forearm. Her arms remain as she continues turning (1/4 more) to face downstage right, her right leg now in *attitude*. While she begins the swivel turn, the man, who has been facing front, walks 'around' her in the same direction, ending with a lunge on his left leg, taking weight on the right knee with his torso leaning far forward (*penché*). During his walk she lets go of his right shoulder and takes his right hand (or wrist, if his arm is long). As the *penché* finishes she turns her head toward the man and he turns his toward her so that their lips are close. There should be only a suggestion of a kiss. The heights of the dancers may cause this moment to be only an intimate look at each other. After a pause she brings her torso upright, as does he. She balances against him, her left hip against his right shoulder area, opening her left arm sideward, her right arm up, while at the same time he slowly places his left hand on his hip, his right arm extending sideward, palm down. They end looking at each other.

Transition to Tirolese

Following the conclusion of the Canzonetta a transition takes place in silence. The Canzonetta dancers turn and walk in a dignified manner to the upstage right chaise. At the same time the Tirolese man moves out from behind the upstage left chaise and stands near the end of it ready to start the next dance. The Tirolese woman gets up from the chaise and takes a few steps away from it, placing herself to balance his location on stage.

Tirolese

The Tirolese is a light, bright dance. Tudor used many familiar ballet steps, but with minor variations which render them more interesting. Much depends on the quality: the use of energy, the emphases in the different sequences, the relationship to space and that of the partners to each other. It is the interplay between these elements that makes this *pas de deux* particularly interesting.

[1-2] Before the music begins the man runs forward to center upstage and offers his right arm, palm up, to his partner - an invitation to join him. She immediately picks up on his intentions and quickly runs to him, crossing behind him to his left side. As she passes him she takes his right hand with her left, and, with a *piqué* on her left foot turning to the right to face upstage, she takes his left hand in her right. At this point both have raised their arms sideward high. This momentary back-to-back position dissolves as, keeping his left hand in her right, she lets go of his right hand and, with a step to get around him, turns to face the audience. The music begins, cueing in as she takes her first *piqué* step, and, once they are facing front (still holding inside hands), the music 'sweeps' them into a forward run toward the audience.

[3-6] In the first two measures the dancers move symmetrically. The step pattern containing a bright *ballonné* and *piqué* takes them first in, toward each other, then away; they separate before coming in toward each other again on [5-6]. The step pattern is most effective when quite significant traveling is achieved on each *piqué* and *ballonné*, so that space is covered and the 'toward and away' idea is stressed. The use of 5 beats and a pause gives character to this phrase, as does the fact that the *croisé* and *effacé* positions are reversed, the *piqué* to low *attitude* being *effacé* when the dancers are separated and *croisé* when they are near each other. These minor differences make this pattern a trifle hard to grasp at once. In addition the arm movements are simple and sparse and do not change as often as would be expected - hence the hold signs in the arm columns at the start of [5 and 7].

[7-10] The first pattern is now repeated; at the end of the repetition the dancers travel even farther apart with a turning *chassé-coupé* into a lunge, both arms directed away from their partner. A slight *fermata* in the music gives the dancers the extra time needed to move in toward each other. The man stops in a diagonal lunge and the woman takes his proffered left hand as she steps into a *piqué* turn to the left, passing behind his back in a manner similar to that of their opening coming together. The woman must be fleet of foot to achieve this sequence, to be ready to move on the beat and to have arrived directly behind her partner to get into the next phrase.

[11-14] As the man performs a gentle *balancé* step, more or less on the spot, holding her left hand in his right, the woman travels around him with a brightly articulated *pas de basque*. With four *pas de basque* she must complete one and a half circles so that she finishes in front of him. To help her achieve this the man moves slightly from side to side to move out of her way as she travels around him.

[15-18] Now facing front, the woman at the left and slightly in front of the man, both travel on a diagonal toward upstage left. As the left foot steps diagonally backward low, the right leg is extended out in a preparation for a *raccourci*, (a pulling in of the right leg to *retiré*) which coincides with the left leg springing into an *élancé* onto *pointe* traveling back in the same direction. A *coupé* over with the right foot completes the step pattern, which is performed four times. The man's *élancé* is, of course, not on *pointe* but to a high 3/4 toe. As the next step is to start with the right foot, the phrase ends with a *fondu* on the left leg instead of the *coupé* over as before.

[19-22] As though enjoying this unison movement, the couple now travels forward the full length of the stage diagonal with four *pas de basque* steps, zig-zagging slightly to the right and left as they progress. The man has his left arm around the woman's waist, his right hand holding her right hand. The woman waves her free arm across at low level on the first *pas de basque* and out to the side on the second, the turn of her head accompanying her arm. The mood is playful, the energy held in reserve.

[23-26] Now the path is reversed and the same *pas de basque* step travels backward. There is a sense of 'marking time'; are they teasing the audience, perhaps saying, "Just wait, something special is coming."

[27-37] Once more they travel forward on the same diagonal, but this time the energy bursts out as both perform a turning *chassé-coupé-grand jeté en avant* ending on the right foot in 1st *arabesque*. The feeling is of darting through space, of piercing it with the right arm as the arm extends forward in *arabesque* line. On landing the *arabesque* position is held, suspended, so that it can really register. A transition step on the left leads into a step-hop-hop on the right foot, the left leg being held in a long front *attitude*, the right hand moving along its length as though caressing it (i.e., brushing it) without quite touching it. For both, the head and body are inclined to the right, the body more forward to accommodate the arm movement. The same step-hop-hop is then performed on the other side, the left hand brushing near the right leg. This pattern travels less and is more introvert, more concerned with self and with showing the elegant line of the leg. Now the energy bursts out again as the *chassé-coupé-jeté* step is repeated, darting through space, but the diagonal space h s been 'consumed', so they turn and run swiftly on the same diagonal to just in front of the upstage left chaise. On arriving the man steps into a lunge on his left leg, his arms extending sideward. With a *piqué* into an *arabesque*, the woman balances with her left hand on his right shoulder, her right hand taking his. With a quick half-turn to the right, she turns under his right arm and takes his left hand with her left as he also turns. There is a moment of suspension, and then both run as fast as possible forward on the same stage diagonal. Tudor's use here of this diagonal is interesting. First the dancers travel along it with the rather gentle *pas de basque*, forward, then backward. Next comes heightened energy as they dart forward along it, the exhilarating turning leap being punctuated by the sensitive 'stroking' of the leg in front *attitude*. A swift run back along the

diagonal is arrested by the *pose* in *arabesque* and the turn which precedes the dash to the downstage right corner.

[38-45] Once more the dancers travel backward on this same stage diagonal, but now they are not in unison and the motif features turning. Holding right hands and gradually traveling upstage, the dancers perform two *balancé* steps, the woman turning under the man's right arm. This is followed by what might be called an inversion of the step in [15 and 16]. The low backward step also precedes an *élancé* backward, but this time the free leg extends as in a *développé* on the *élancé* before the *coupé* over which follows. The two *balancés* and the two *élancé* patterns are then repeated so that the dancers finish as far back as possible.

[46-53] Now comes what could be called the 'grand tour of the salon'. The spatial restriction of the diagonal line is abandoned in favor of the largest possible circle (in fact, an incomplete circle). The step is a return to the *pas de basque* of [19-22], but now performed more robustly, the woman's free arm weaving to and fro at a higher level, the dancers' upper bodies turning first toward each other, then away. The woman's arm movements may be performed as a long horizontal figure eight. On the seventh *pas de basque* the dancers spiral in, having arrived in the downstage left corner. Standing on the left leg, facing *croisé* they pause, hands on hips, looking at each other as though to say, "What next?".

[54-57] There follows what might be called a little conversation, quite small movement in contrast to the preceding phrases. Traveling to stage right the man performs three *chassé-coupé-ballonnés*. On each *chassé* the man opens his right arm out in a curved gesture as though saying, "Come over here"; on the *ballonné* he returns his right hand to his hip. The third time there is no *ballonné*; instead he springs into an open 4th position and then quickly springs into the other 4th, turning to face his partner, his left arm opening out to her in a gesture of invitation as he looks at her.

[58-61] The woman responds by repeating the man's step of [54] twice; the third *chassé-coupé* leads into an *assemblé* into 5th position landing facing upstage next to the man on his left and ending with a spring *relevé*. The man, now facing the audience, closes into 5th and *relevés* in the same 5th position as the woman. Facing in opposite directions, each has the left hand at the partner's waist, the right arm up, and each looks at the other.

[62-69] While the man does two *balancé* steps on the spot starting with the left foot and turning to the left, the woman makes just over a half-circle around him with two *pas de basque* steps also starting left; each dancer waves the raised right arm 'overhead' across to the left side on the first step and out to the side on the second. Ending facing downstage left, the woman now 'shoots' into that direction with a step on the left foot into a *cabriole croisée en avant,* her traveling being helped by a boost from the man who, having quickly turned into the same direction, places his right hand on the left-back-diagonal part of her chest, giving her a push forward just as she rises into the air. At the same time he steps toward her and grasps her left hand in his left. As she 'flies' away from him the man lets go of her left hand, and then takes it with his right as he takes another step toward her. After landing from the *cabriole,* the woman takes a long *chassé* step forward on the right foot into a *relevé* in 1st *arabesque croisée,* her right palm up. For a moment they remain still, registering the long line extending from her right arm to his left. The woman then must perform a very quick catch step onto her

left foot as she turns to face stage right to circle around him again with two more *pas de basque* steps, her right hand held in his, her free left arm waving across and then out to the side. Arriving facing upstage after the second *pas de basque*, she steps into an *assemblé devant* turning to face the audience, and ending with a spring *relevé* in 5th as before. After performing two *balancé* steps in place, slowly turning to the right with his left hand on his hip, the man also does an *assemblé* turning to finish facing upstage, left foot front, ending with a spring *relevé* in 5th. The position is exactly as in [61], but the dancers are now facing the other way. The entire pattern [62-69] is now performed again identically, but placed in the opposite direction on stage, the woman shooting forward toward upstage right. On the *assemblé* the man turns so that both dancers end facing the audience, holding inside hands.

[78-81] Moving away from each other and using opposite feet, each dancer performs a sideward *chassé-coupé* turn ending facing front again with a sideward step leaving the free foot in *pointe tendue* with the arms out. They pause for a moment before a tiny spring and a tap, reiterating the *pointe tendue* to which they draw attention by leaning toward that foot and looking at it. The foot is immediately 'snatched' into 5th *relevé*, right foot front, as the body and head come upright. Now a quick half-turn takes place so that this *pointe tendue* is done on the other side facing upstage. On the *relevé* in 5th, however, there is another quick half-turn to face front. This foot pattern requires quick articulation, and contrasts with the larger movement sequences that preceded it. This 'perky' interlude *sur place* is followed by a traveling step.

[82-89] Traveling in opposite directions, the dancers perform a *chassé-coupé-ballonné* step similar to that in [54], the arm gesture opening out and returning to the hip in the same manner. The step is repeated for a total of four times as the dancers curve around to meet upstage slightly left of center. The man, now facing upstage right, lunges on his left foot, arms outstretched in 2nd, to provide a steady base for the woman who, facing the same direction, takes a *piqué* step into *arabesque*, placing her right hand on his right wrist, her left hand on his right shoulder. She pauses there a moment before whipping her leg out and into a *pirouette en dedans*, 'catching' the man again for support as she does a *développé* forward which is followed by a back bend, her head turned to the left to look at the audience. She steps out of this and he changes weight to his right foot just before the next phrase begins.

[90-98] With the woman on the man's right, their left hands holding, his right arm around her waist, the couple begins a wide half-circle around the stage, ending downstage center. Two preparatory *pas de basque* steps starting on the left foot lead into a full *chassé-coupé* turn for her as a preparation for a high *saut de basque* for which the man, taking the woman's right hand in his, gives her a boost so that she 'sails' around. The man accommodates his steps to her need, traveling forward while she is in the air. The woman takes her right arm out to the side and then forward to her partner. The taking of right hands occurs as they face each other, arms across the body, and allows the arms to open out and up as the man helps lift and turn the woman with a circular arm movement overhead. Depending on heights, length of arms, etc., some dancers achieve this boosted lift more easily than others. The two *pas de basque*, the preparation and the lift are repeated again. At the conclusion the dancers face front, standing still in 5th position, arms out to the sides. The man is on the right and they are enough apart to provide room for the next step.

[99-106] The couple repeat identically the opening theme, i.e., [3 - start of 10]. The steps are now more exaggerated, the front *attitude* legs are lifted higher with the body leaning away from the *attitude* leg.

[107-114] The man now repeats the *chassé-coupé-ballonné* step of [54-57], but traveling to the left toward his partner. Again he ends with a small spring from 4th to 4th. The woman responds with a series of six *petits jetés* traveling sideward toward him, facing front, her arms out to the side, the lower arms up. Stepping to the right and turning in toward him, she does a *coupé* under, turning to face front and springing into a front *attitude*, the right leg lifted, arms up in 5th. As she springs the man grasps her waist and lifts her as high as possible, holding her there long enough to establish the end of the dance.

Transition to Bolero

The Tirolese man swiftly puts his partner down, both then turn to face upstage left and run to the upstage left chaise where they sit down. Meanwhile the Bolero women, B1, B2, B3, rise and, with B1 leading and the others taking their cue from her, walk in a stately manner to their places. Stepping forward on the right foot, they place the left leg in a forward *pointe tendue*, the leg bent, both legs turned out, the torso high, the chest well lifted, the arms in 4th and the gaze far forward. Inner strength shows through the eyes as though to hypnotize the audience. This pose sets the tone, the dynamic for the dance that follows. This carriage of torso and head should be featured throughout the piece, particularly in the simpler steps and moments of pause, it should not, however, become static or rigid. There will be some natural lessening at times with a return to the more pronounced uplift and energy. Such slight variations are not given in the notation.

Bolero

[1-4] The first unison step has an almost mesmerizing effect. The interplay between timing, transference of weight, the opening and closing of the leg gesture accompanied by only one arm, gives the 12-count phrase a particular character. The seeming repetition is broken in a subtle and unexpected way. The *pointes tendues* are crisp, the undulating arm gestures are quick but not sharp. While the dancers progress forward and the right foot and right arm move laterally, the raised left arm remains motionless and the gaze continues to penetrate forward. The slower transference of weight onto the left foot in *plié* and the pause that follows are contrasted by the quick out-in-out *pointes tendues*. This phrase ends with a step so that the step in *plié* on the left foot can be repeated. It is now followed by a rise as the right leg extends to the side before a *coupé* over-*coupé* under pattern ends with a lone *pointe tendue* to the side. A step forward on the right foot leads into a repeat of this 12-count phrase. At the end of the repeat of these twelve counts the *coupé* behind on the left foot becomes the start of a *pas de bourrée* for which the arms open out and change to the opposite 4th position.

[5-7] Forming a small circle with the right shoulder to the center, the three dancers walk on the circular line, first with backward steps, then turning outward as they travel so that they end with forward steps. These steps are on *pointe* with parallel legs, the foot picked up into a low

parallel *retiré* on each step. The last (6th) step is on *pointe* on a *fondu* with the torso leaning backward. The arms are placed in front of the body on the dancer's center line, the right starting higher than the left. So that the arms follow the circular design, the upper body begins twisted to the right, hands on the circular line; then, as the dancers turn on the circular path, their arms, as though 'leading' into the circling, move outward and cause a twist to the left in the body, the hands of each ending on the circular line near the back of the woman in front. Having arrived at the original place of the woman in front (one third of a circle being achieved), the dancers reverse the pattern. The marked lift in the body (which continues through most of this dance) is contrasted by the hand position in which the hands 'droop' forward, palms 'down' (i.e., facing backward). This is the first real indication of Tudor's tongue-in-cheek humor in this choreography, although there is a suspicion of it in the opening step sequence. Reversing the direction of travel and changing again from backward steps to forward steps, the dancers again 'lead' the circling with their arms, ending with the upper body twisted to the right. The last step is off *pointe* and the legs turn out in preparation for the end of this phrase. Now facing downstage right, all *coupé* under on *pointe* taking the right foot into a high *retiré*, right arm up and left arm and head focus out to the left side. This position is held and then a small spring into a 4th *ouvert* position onto the whole foot provides the cadence to this phrase.

[8-9] Now comes a series of tap-steps all performed on *pointe*, with the knees always slightly bent. The change in rhythm and in direction make this sequence tricky to learn. Against the rhythmic footwork pattern the arms move in a sustained manner from one *croisé* 4th position opening out into the other. On the up-beat there is a *fondu* on the right leg as the left leg gestures to the side in preparation for a step-*croisé* on count 1. Then follow two tapping gestures by the right foot as the leg circles inward. During the two taps on '2 &' there is a turn to the left, so that the step which follows on the right foot on count 3 is also *croisé*. On the next step-tap-step-tap starting on the left foot ('4 & 5 &') there is a turn to the right, so that the final forward step on the left is again *croisé*. The same rhythmic step pattern is now repeated on the other foot but starts *effacé* - a more difficult pattern because the first part of this repeat has no turning motion to help the circular leg gesture in performing the taps. However the phrase ends as before, with the exception that after the last *croisé* step there is a small spring in the air into an *assemblé* which is the start of the next pattern.

[10-11] The *assemblé* lands in a 5th *croisé plié*, the left foot front and the torso tilted well forward, arms in *bras bas* near the feet. A limping pattern follows, the left foot 'limping' forward on *pointe* with a bent leg, the right picking up behind and quickly replacing the left. The sequence ends with a *coupé* over on the left foot into a *fondu*. During four limping steps, the dancers turn three-quarters to the right to face downstage left; at the same time on each limp the hands make little forward circles as the arms gradually rise. The head focuses all the while on the left foot. There is a faint air of the ridiculous in this step, with the arms rising, the torso remaining tilted forward, and the seeming frivolity of the hand circles. In complete contrast to the smallness of these movements the next phrase contains long, extended movements which delineate the spatial line between downstage left and upstage right. A right step backward on *pointe* precedes the left leg unfolding to forward high as the torso tilts way back, the upper body twisted to the right, the arms directed in line with the left leg, with the head looking up along the same line. Now comes a very fast turn during two quick steps traveling toward the downstage left corner. During the turn the torso retains its spatial

direction (as in a barrel roll) so that it ends tilted forward toward upstage right. The supporting right leg sinks deeper and the left leg points backward continuing the line of the body. The left arm is in 5th overhead, the right is backward and the head is turned looking at the right hand. This position needs to be established and clearly held for a moment before the dancer makes a sudden half-turn to face downstage left again and travel forward with two low steps on *pointe*. Again the torso retains its spatial direction during the turn so that it is again leaning backward, but now with the pelvis thrust forward. The arms are forward, the left higher than the right, hands 'limp' as when the dancers moved around in the small circles [5]. The head now focuses on the audience, and is not - as might be expected - in line with the body.

[12-15] The tap-step now reappears, but starts *croisé* on the right foot and turns to the right first. After the first six counts, the step changes to a slow 'picked up' *pas de bourrée dessous*, the dancers starting with the left foot and ending facing the audience, left foot 5th front. At the start of the *pas de bourrée* the arms are sideward, the lower arms raised forming a slight angle, palms facing in. As the foot closes into 5th the torso lifts strongly out of the hips, the rib cage expanded, the head focus far forward. This position is held for counts 4, 5, 6. On the next count 1 there is a deep *fondu* on the front foot, the right leg extending far back to *pointe tendue*. The torso is well stretched forward parallel with the floor, the neck long, the face looking down, the arms out to the sides, bent and rotated inward. This pose is held for two counts, before a low swiveling turn during which the weight is taken onto the back foot and the left foot slides on the toe, the body coming upright. The swivel turn ends with the dancers facing downstage right, the left leg ending *pointe tendue* toward stage left, arms gesturing toward stage right and head focusing toward the audience. This position is held very briefly, before a *rond de jambe* of the left leg sliding on the floor initiates a turn to face the back in order to start a stately, paced walk upstage, the arms held in 1st until after the 5th step when there is a swift turn to face front. The phrase concludes with the right leg *pointe tendue* forward with a bent knee, arms out to the side, lower arms angled upward, palms facing in, a pose which is held only briefly.

[16-22] Now comes the 'Petal Pattern'. As illustrated in the floor plan the circular paths of the three dancers overlap slightly to form the petals of a flower. In performing this design it is not easy to start and to maintain the appropriate curves, since the step pattern is somewhat complex. No corners should be cut. The sequence starts with a *piqué* step forward on the right foot, the left leg raised into a low front extension, the chest inclined slightly forward over the leg. The left arm is also over the left leg, and that hand performs an outward circle ending with the palm up, the focus being on the hand. After stepping forward on a *demi-plié*, the same pattern is repeated, but enlarged. The second *piqué* step on the right leg leads to a hip-high forward gesture for the left, the torso now leaning more prominently over that leg, the arm rising as two inward circles are performed by the left lower leg and by the hand. These embellished gestures conclude with a low step forward while the arm is carried out to the side. Next, starting with the right foot, there follows an up-up, down-down, up-up walking pattern, performed with long steps, the legs being very stretched on the high steps. During these six steps the arms which start in close to the body, near the front of the chest, extend forward and outward with outward rotation in one continuous sweeping movement. At the start of this walk the head is inclined to the left and turned slightly to the right and remains there. These two measures are repeated, the hands of the dancers coming close together as the end of the individual circles bring the dancers near each other. Next comes a continuous low walk with

nine very long steps during which the arms again open out from near the chest, but this time with the torso leaning diagonally back to the left. On this low walk the dancers move apart into one large circle, ending with B1 upstage center, B2 and B3 in the downstage left and right corners. The phrase ends with a *piqué* step across on the left foot into an *en dehors pirouette*, which finishes in a 4th position lunge facing downstage right, arms forward, hands again 'drooped', the right above the left, the neck long, the focus to the audience. With barely any pause the dancers swivel on both feet into the opposite 4th position ending in a lunge facing downstage left. As they turn, their arms draw in slightly and then extend out again with the left hand above the right.

[23-26] The dance now returns to the opening step, performed exactly as before except that B2 and B3 reverse it by traveling backward. The ending of [26] provides a transition into the next section. B1 takes a low step across with the left foot into a *relevé* turn, the right leg opening into a diagonal *développé* as the body leans away from it, the focus being upward in the direction of the leg. This *effacé* position is sustained for a moment before she turns and runs swiftly on a curve upstage, ending near the right hand chaise to be in position for a long diagonal line for her solo. As she arrives she turns to face downstage left just in time to start her first step. The transition for the other women is simpler. B2 takes a *demi-plié* in 5th left foot front, arms in *bras bas*, then springs into *relevé* in 5th, arms rising to 5th. She then sinks into a 4th position *croisé* lunge, the upper body tilted slightly to the right, arms opening out to the sides, in line with the shoulders, palms up. B3 performs this same transition to the other side. All during B1's solo she performs B2's movements in lateral symmetry.

Solo for B1

[27-30] The movements in this solo are broad, making full use of space both in traveling and in the expansive arm gestures. Starting on the left foot, two low steps lead into a big *grand jeté en avant* with full *port de bras* to 5th, the focus being forward high. This *jeté* suspends in the air (if the dancer can achieve it). On landing on the left foot, she sinks to her right knee (weight divided between foot and knee) as her arms open into a wide, generous 1st *arabesque*-like position, left arm forward, right arm backward, both rounded, with palms up, the upper body leaning to the right, the focus still up. Her right arm then sweeps down and the left arm opens sideward as it moves back, as they change into a rounded 2nd *arabesque*, palms up [28]. It is the right arm transition that is emphasized and hence featured. During this movement the head inclines and turns to the right toward the audience. The '*largesse*' of these curved

B2; B3

[27-30] With hands held as though they are playing castanets, the two women perform a slow *port de bras*. B2 inclines her chest to the right as her right arm lowers to *bras bas*; as this arm comes forward and up to 5th she inclines to the left; as it moves out to 2nd she comes upright. This two-measure full *port de bras* is then repeated. B3 performs the movement of B2 in lateral symmetry, circling her left arm.

movements is now contrasted by the swiftness that follows in which spoke-like arm movements pierce the air. Placing the weight forward on the left foot, B1 starts to turn, taking another fast step to complete a half-turn traveling toward downstage left, ending in a low *fondu* with her left leg *pointe tendue* far backward. During these turning steps the arms draw in and then extend out, the left one up, the right out to the side. At the same time the chest is inclined and twisted to the right so that head focus and right arm gesture relate to the audience. This twist in the body is maintained as the left foot steps back into a half-turn, the dancer ending facing downstage left, her right leg swiftly moving to *pointe tendue* forward. Once more the arms draw in on the step and turn, extending this time to the forward position with hands 'drooping', the right above the left; the head turned to the left, looking in the direction of downstage left but tilted backward, an opposition movement to the chest twist to the right. A quick shift onto the right foot allows the whole two-measure phrase to be repeated to the same side.

Solo for B1

[31-34] At the end of the previous phrase B1 takes a very fast '*glissade*' to the right as a preparation into a suspended *piqué* to an open *arabesque effacée* toward downstage right, her arms high to the sides but well rounded, the hands rotating outward as she establishes the pose. She suspends for the counts 2-5, stepping across on count 6 to take a *piqué* step to the right side facing front, the left leg coming to a high *retiré*. The arms, having lowered slightly, hands returned to normal, now rise again, the hands again rotating outward, this time with a slight accent. Suspending this pose for the rest of the measure, she sinks taking the left foot backward into a long *croisé* 4th position lunge, the start of a slow swivel

B2; B3

[31-34] Facing downstage left B2 rises into 5th *croisé*, right foot front, arms in 5th. On count 4 she takes her left leg backward into a lunge as her body tilts to the left, her arms in an open angular sideward position, palms facing in. This pattern is repeated on the other side, facing downstage right. Then a *grand port de bras* follows, the torso inclining way forward and then the chest inclining backward, the whole *port de bras* taking a total of twelve counts.

turn. At the start the torso inclines to the right as the upper body twists to the left. Her right arm comes in to the body and, led by the front of the chest, unfolds toward the audience, as though addressing them, until it becomes carried around with her as, with both supports now low, the swivel turn progresses. Ending facing downstage right, with weight on the left leg, B1 takes four long slow deliberate steps on the 'measured' music, first backward, then toward downstage left as she turns to face that direction. She ends on her left foot and makes an active *pointe tendue en arrière* with the right as her arms change majestically to a high 4th position.

Solo for B1

[35-38] Facing downstage right to start a large circular path around the stage, B1 performs a demanding pattern of steps almost all on *pointe*, turning around herself on the circular path. The start of this pattern is like the 'tap-step' of [8], but the dancer moves forward on the right foot, the two taps making a *rond de jambe* into a crossed diagonal step on the left foot, leading into a *pas de bourrée* under turning to the right. The *pas de bourrée* ends with a low step forward on the right whole foot, this being the preparation for a *jeté en avant* onto *pointe* on a bent left leg, the free leg being lifted to *arabesque*. During the tap-step the arms open and change to a high 4th, the right arm up; for the *pas de bourrée*, the arms come down down and are carried forward rounded to extend forward with palms up as the *jeté* lands. If possible the long line between *arabesque* leg and arms extended forward should be clearly registered before the whole 6-count phrase is repeated again. It takes four repeats of this phrase to make the full circular path.

B2; B3

[35-39] After the sustained 'soothing' *port de bras*, these two dancers begin a more Spanish-style step. Facing downstage right, B2 takes a low step across (preceded by an unobtrusive shift of weight to the right foot), extending her right leg diagonally forward, her right arm diagonally up, her head focus in the same line. As the lower leg does two *ronds de jambe en dehors*, the right hand makes two circles in a similar manner. Turning to downstage left, she grasps her skirt and does a *tombé* into a low crossed step which leads into a 'picked up' *pas de bourrée* under as she turns to face downstage right again, bringing her skirt across to end with a low crossed diagonal step. With a quick change of front she turns to face downstage left, releasing her skirt before repeating this 6-count phrase to the other side, performing it alternately for a total of four times. Note that there is no *relevé* on the *rond de jambe* as might be expected.

[39-41] The three dancers now move in unison as they sweep clockwise around the stage with nine very long, low steps (similar to [20]), the arms again starting from near the

chest to move forward and slightly outward, with much outward rotation. The circling closes in so that they end fairly close together upstage center. The last step is a preparation for a double *en dedans piqué pirouette* with all three ending facing downstage right as the right foot steps backward into a *croisé* 4th position lunge, arms forward, hands limp, the right wrist above the left, the face toward the audience. Holding this position only for a moment, the dancers swivel to the right to end facing downstage left in the opposite *croisé* 4th position lunge, the arms drawing in as they turn and extending again on the lunge with the left wrist now above the right. This concluding position is held until the opening theme in the music returns.

[42-48] As expected, the three dancers repeat in unison the four measures of the opening steps, but with an increased intensity as though saying "We've told you this already". This phrase again ends with forming a small circle, but now the circle starts traveling clockwise, one third of the way around, with only forward steps, the arms again 'leading', the right above the left, the hands 'limp', as before. With a *fondu* on the 6th step, the dancers change traveling direction, now walking backward six steps with a *fondu* on the last step. Right after this last step all turn to face the audience with a *piqué* under on the right foot into a high *retiré*, the arms in 1st. Holding this position for a moment, each then turns to take her final pose. B1 turns to upstage left, lunging on the left leg into a kneel, the upper body turned and inclined toward the audience, the right arm curved around the head which is looking at the audience. B2 changes weight to face downstage left, her right leg bent in a *croisé pointe tendue,* her left hand on her hip, her right arm up in 5th, her head looking to the audience. B3 is in lateral symmetry to B2.

Transition to Neapolitan

B1, B2 and B3 turn to face upstage and walk with measured pace (keeping in character) to their places on the chaises. In the meantime MC rises to his feet and walks to the left around the end of the right chaise to stand behind it, thus giving his place to B2. MT rises, steps to the other end of his (the left) chaise and sits at that end, thus giving his previous seat to B3. N rises and walks to the left side of the chaise, taking a pose on her left foot with arms out sideward, open in a wide angle. MN takes a similar pose near the right side of the upstage right chaise.

Neapolitan

Note that until [65] the movement phrases in this dance start in the middle of a measure, hence the indication of the half-measure. The dancers' counts in sets of eight start on the second half of each measure. The music is 12/8, giving four main beats to each measure.

[1-3½] With a light run, the free leg kicked out backward and bent, N and MN (her partner) cross one another and make a large circle around the stage with ten runs, the attention-seeking 'shaking' (rotating) of their hands adding to the fun. Note that because the entire two runs cut into the third measure the dancers' phrase from there on commences in the middle of each music measure.

[3½-5] In the first step pattern which begins halfway through the third measure, they face in toward each other and move symmetrically. Facing downstage left the woman steps across with her right foot, as a preparation for a *coupé* under into a *grand rond de jambe sauté* into *attitude* turning to the right; this turning continues with a swift *pas de bourrée* under closing right foot 5th front. This closing becomes the preparation for a *sissonne en avant* toward downstage right, the phrase ending with a *chassé croisé* into a lunge forward on the left leg. At the start, to assist the turn and give lift for the *sauté*, the right arm comes across before opening out into 2nd and then rises overhead on a curved path deviating slightly backward. The left arm moves in opposition, lowering as the right arm moves up; both end in 1st before opening side low for the *pas de bourrée*; they then pass through *bras bas* on their way forward to arrive in a pose at the end of the phrase. In this pose the torso is leaning right diagonally forward, the arms are rounded in the same direction, the right higher than the left, both with 'lifted' elbows (inward rotation of the elbows); the head inclines to the right but is turned to the left (i.e., toward the audience). During this whole sequence MN moves symmetrically to N.

[5½-9] The next movement phrase, which starts in the middle of [5], features N circling to the left with four hops on the right leg, the left leg performing a *rond de jambe* on each hop. The left arm is low across the body, the right arm diagonally right back low as the chest inclines to the left, and the focus is on the left foot. MN does the same pattern to the other side. Concluding with an *assemblé*, left foot front, the woman contrasts the previous small rapid leg movements with a high *entrechat six* with full *port de bras* ending with arms up. In contrast the man uses the landing in the *assemblé* as a preparation for a double *pirouette* to the right, ending on his right knee, his right arm diagonally forward to the woman, his left out to the side, both palms up. Taking the man's proffered right hand with her left, the woman circles around him counterclockwise with eight traveling *ballonnés*.

[9½-11] Still holding the man's hand, the woman takes a *piqué* into *attitude effacée* facing downstage left, then a *fondu* into a *piqué attitude effacée* on the right foot. An *assemblé en arrière* is the preparation for a double *pirouette* to the right closing fifth behind. As she performs the *assemblé* the man rises onto his left foot into an *assemblé en arrière* which for him is a preparation for an *entrechat six* with full *port de bras*.

[11½-15] An identical repeat of the first step pattern of [3½-5] now follows, the man's arms ending up as his right foot closes behind at the end of his *pirouette*.

[15½-19] A crossing step now follows, the dancers traveling to stage left and stage right, the man performing the opposite to the woman. Before crossing, each takes a *piqué* to *arabesque effacée* away from the other, the woman having her right arm up, her left hand at her hip. Two traveling steps prepare for a *grand jeté en tournant* with full *port de bras*. Two more traveling steps lead into a rhythmic step circling on the spot. In this step the right foot is always in front for the woman and the arms are held out to the side in line with the shoulders, the elbows slightly bent. While circling to the left the woman drops onto her left foot in *fondu* [17½, count 1], the right *cou de pied* in front, her chest leaning toward the supporting foot. Two fast steps on the spot on *pointe* follow (count 2 '&') then a drop onto the right foot, the left *cou de pied* behind, her chest now leaning to the right (count 3). Two more fast steps on *pointe* (count 4 '&') lead into a repeat which ends on count 7, count 8 being held.

[19½-23] A symmetrical repeat of the *piqué* to *arabesque effacée*, the crossing and the circling in place now occurs, ending on count 7 of [23], count 8 being held. As before, the dancers have exchanged places, the woman now being near the downstage right corner, the man the downstage left corner.

[23½-25] The next phrase of eight counts takes the dancers back to the upstage left corner, their paths crossing at the end (see floor plan) so that the man ends on the woman's right. It is almost as though they run to see who can get to the upstage left corner first. The traveling step is the same for both - a simple run-run-step-*grand jeté en avant* in 2nd *arabesque* performed twice. As she leaps the woman looks at the man, and continues looking at him until she turns swiftly to get into the next step. He also looks at her. For the man the transition into the next step involves a half-turn during the second *jeté* so that his right leg ends forward instead of backward; his arms close in on the turn and then end side. Both are now facing downstage right to start the next step.

[25½-29] Traveling together on the diagonal to downstage right, the couple perform different, but somewhat complementary steps.

N

The woman hops continuously forward on her left leg, her right foot touching first *pointe tendue* forward, then across in front and to the left of her left foot. Her right arm is across her body as her torso leans forward toward her right foot. Her focus is toward this foot. After the eighth hop she faces front, does a *relevé devant* on her left leg, right arm in front, her chest leaning toward the raised leg. She then closes in 5th front *plié* as a preparation for a *relevé derrière*, changing the arms and leaning toward the left leg. Closing her left foot behind in *plié* becomes the preparation for a double *pirouette en dehors* to the right, at the end of which her right leg extends forward at hip level before closing in 5th front, the arms opening with the leg, ending in the 'greeting' position, palms up.

MN

Traveling close by her side, also facing downstage right, the man steps forward on his right foot into a series of traveling hops in *arabesque*. During the six counts his arms rise slowly forward in 3rd *arabesque*; his head is turned to look at the woman. Closing his left leg into 5th behind with a little spring (count 7), he then does two high 'stag' jumps, each staying in the air for a whole count (counts 8 and 2). In the first one his right leg is in *retiré*, the left extended backward into an *arabesque* line, his upper body bent toward that leg. Both arms are lifted diagonally to the right, with the lower arms twisted outward, (palms 'up'), his focus being in the same direction. This jump lands 5th left front and is then repeated to the other side facing downstage left. Landing right 5th front is followed by a *relevé* facing front - the preparation for a double *tour en l'air* which ends right foot 5th behind with the arms open in a 'greeting' gesture, palms up.

In performing this passage the partners have to be near each other for the hops and then far enough apart so that the man has room for his spectacular jumps. The passage works best if on his last hop the man moves to be slightly away and upstage of her.

[29½-37] Turning to face downstage right, both dancers repeat this phrase of sixteen counts twice more.

[37½-39] Side by side but facing at an angle away from each other, both *relevé croisé* in preparation for a *plié* and an *entrechat six* which turns them to face the opposite corner, toward each other, again in *croisé*. During the *relevé* hands are on the hips; for the *six* they perform an upward *port de bras*, arms ending sideward. The *relevé* and the *entrechat six* are repeated.

[39½-41] Facing downstage right, the man now steps backward on his right foot, taking his left foot to *pointe tendue* backward. He places the back of his left hand on his hip and extends his right arm upward in a long *arabesque* line. With her right foot the woman takes a long, low, slow *chassé* forward close to him and, as she rises into *attitude*, takes his right hand with her left inclining her body to the right, her head looking toward the audience under her left arm. Holding that position for one count (4), she then lowers while turning to the left and bringing her arms down as she takes two steps walking around the man, who closes his left foot into 1st (to get it out of her way, since she needs to remain very close to him to get around to his right side). Facing downstage right, she takes a *piqué* forward on her left foot into *attitude*, her torso pitched forward, her right arm up holding the man's right hand as she twists her upper body to the left to look at him. As she does the *piqué* he lowers on his right leg into a 4th position lunge and looks at her.

Transition to Finale

[41½-51] Both dancers break away from this 'togetherness' and begin what is, in effect, a calling of the other dancers to join in the Finale, which begins without any interruption as a continuation of the Neapolitan dance. With the same springing run as at the start of their duet, arms out, hands 'fluttering', the dancers travel with eight steps toward the chaises. As they pass the other dancers they perform a step-*cabriole en arrière*, raising the inside arm up in a calling, 'come on' gesture. After a quick half-turn the *cabriole* and arm gesture are repeated on the other side. After another half-turn the two *cabrioles* and two arm gestures are repeated again. During these steps the couple pass along the length of the nearest chaise. They then repeat the running pattern as each moves to the next chaise, where they repeat the 'calling' step four more times. The dancers then travel along the edge of the stage with a *chassé-coupé*-turning step to meet downstage center, where, facing each other, they pause on the left foot, the right *pointe tendue derrière*. While they travel downstage the other dancers indicate their interest in joining, rise and run to their places, forming with N and MN a large circle around the stage. T and MT face one another, C faces B1, while MC faces B2. At first B3 is on her own between MT and B2.

Finale

[51½-53] With each pair fairly close together, they perform spring points, all using the right foot, and leaning over toward the working foot, the right arm across the body. On the first hop the forward pointing foot is near the other person's foot, on the next hop the foot is brought in to point across to the left in front of the supporting leg. These two spring points are repeated;

then each dancer makes a swift half-turn and, traveling as much as possible to get close to the new partner, repeats the spring points and body position to the other side. This adjustment to get close to the new partner is not easy; it takes two traveling hops to cover the space between.

Women (C, T, N, B1, B2, B3)

[53½-56] The women now turn to face the center of the circle, moving in closer to each other with three steps (L, R, L) ending with a hop in front *attitude*, the right leg and left arm raised, the body inclining toward the supporting foot. Turning with their backs to the center, they repeat the step-hop pattern to the other side moving outward. The stage left dancers (N, T, B3) perform a *soutenu* turn to the left with arms up ending in a forward lunge on the right foot as they lower to the left knee, arms in 1st *arabesque* position, right arm forward, palm up. The women on stage right (C, B1, B2) take a quick catch step on the left foot to do the *soutenu* turn to the right, ending on the right knee. All women hold this position for seven counts.

Women

[57½-59] Starting on [58], the women get up and run on curved paths to their new places: C, N and T to their partners, the Bolero women (B1, B2, B3) into a line upstage between the chaises with B1 in the middle. They stand facing downstage right with the left leg bent in a *pointe tendue croisée,* hands on hips, looking at the audience. They hold this position until [69].

Men (MC, MT, MN)

[53½-57] Turning with their backs to the center of the circle, the men perform the same 'three steps and a hop' pattern, traveling outward at first, then inward to the center. Then, all turning to the right to face upstage, the men take two preparatory steps into a *grand jeté* in 2nd *arabesque* onto the left foot, arms extended, the front arm raised higher than usual. They repeat this pattern to the other side, arriving upstage.

Men

[57½-59] All the men now face stage right, and with a step on the left foot perform a step into a high *fouetté sauté* with full *port de bras* overhead, ending with the arms in 1st *arabesque*. With a hop transition on the left foot the *fouetté sauté* is repeated to the other side. During these seven counts the men must travel downstage as much as possible; this requires practice.

Three Couples (N, MN, C, MC, T, MT)

[59½-61] Facing front, the partners immediately start a quick half *emboîté* step traveling forward. The women extend their left legs on a *fondu* and quickly close in to 5th front on *pointe*, arms out to the side, head looking toward the left foot and then toward the audience as the foot closes in 5th. Releasing the right foot, they place it in front of the left to repeat the *fondu* and the low sideward extension of the left leg. The men perform the same step to the other side, starting with a step on the left in front of the right as they turn to face the audience. For the men, this half *emboîté* step - small, quick, 'tight', almost 'fussy' contrasts strongly with the large traveling *grand jetés* and *fouetté sauté* steps just performed.

[61½-63] For the three couples the movement now opens out into elongated lines, the women taking a *piqué* on the left foot to a high 1st *arabesque* toward downstage left, each man extending his right arm across to the left to take his partner's right hand. Each woman then takes two long steps toward stage right, passing in front of the man in preparation for a repeat to the other side of the *piqué* to 1st *arabesque*, the man then taking her left hand. The woman again takes two long steps, this time toward stage left, to pass in front of her partner.

[63½-66] All three couples now turn left to face upstage, the man on the woman's left with his right arm around her waist. They then do three *chassé coupés* traveling upstage (a 6-count phrase) ending fairly close together to form a trio facing in to one another. The men then lift the women high 'overhead', each woman rising in a 'stag leap' pose, the right leg backward, arms lifted and rounded, the upper body arched backward. In this pose the women's lifted hands are near one another. MC and MT put their partners down first and run with them to the front corners of the stage. MN delays, putting his partner down at the end of [66]. While putting her down he turns to face front, while N ends facing upstage. Note that this 6-count phrase has caused the dancers' movement phrases to coincide with the music bar lines.

From here on the Bolero women join in the activity and the Finale reaches its climax.

N, MN

[67-72] Facing upstage but traveling downstage, N performs a *coupé* under with her right foot followed by a *ballonné* under with the left leg, the step and hop both being on *pointe*. Her arms are held up out to the sides in the wide angle used at the start of the Neapolitan, her body inclining toward the working leg. This step is performed alternately twelve times. MN, who is facing N with his arms in the same pose, performs a series of small step-hop sideward *cabrioles*, starting on the left foot and alternating sides. As he faces front and starts with a *cabriole* to the right, his working leg is parallel to his partner's.

C, MC; T, MT

[67-72] Side by side, the women face front, the men face upstage. C and MC start with their right shoulders close; T, MT perform the same as C, MC, but to the other side starting with left shoulders close, i.e., the partner on the left. The couples now travel upstage with a low step-hop-hop-hop in 2nd *arabesque*, the women stepping and traveling backward, the men forward. After a quick half-turn toward the partner they repeat the pattern, the women now traveling forward, the men backward. These two measures then repeat; each time the half-turn is toward the partner. Arriving near the chaises, these couples face front (the men having done a

B1, B2, B3

[67-72] Now coming into action after having been quiet for several measures, the Bolero women *piqué* forward *croisé* on the left foot into a big *rond de jambe en dedans* with the right leg, the knee slightly bent, at the same time turning to face downstage left. They conclude the circular leg gesture with a lower leg *rond de jambe en dedans* which ends with a slight upward accent. The right arm also makes a high circle *en dedans,* the lower arm circling inward (shown as a backward somersault path) echoing the circling of the foot. Coming off *pointe*, they perform two *croisé* 'limping' steps, the right foot taking a low step forward on *pointe*, the left

quick half-turn) and perform a lateral step pattern, the partners crossing with a sideward step-hop-hop-hop, the women moving out to the side of the stage while the men travel inward passing behind their partners. As they pass each takes his partner's inside hand and the partners look toward each other as they separate. This pattern is repeated to the other side, the women again crossing in front.

closing in with a *coupé* under. During these two 'limping' steps the right hand picks up the previous pattern of the lower arm, making two large inward circles. This *rond de jambe* phrase is repeated twice, each time to the other side (a total of three phrases). The women remain side by side fairly close together while zigzagging toward downstage.

N, MN

[73-77] Having arrived close to the front of the stage, N and MN now zigzag backward with three high lifts to end center stage. Facing downstage right the woman steps and swings her arms to the right, rising into a *pas de poisson*-like hop, her legs bent diagonally backward to the left, her arms across to the right, the right arm higher than the left, both arms rounded. The man lifts her so high that she barely has time to come down and take two fast steps to prepare for the same lift to the other side. This lift is performed three times. At the end of the third lift [75] the woman steps to the left into a *soutenu* turn *en dedans* on *pointe*, her arms making a full *port de bras* to 5th. During this turn her part-

C, MC; T, MT ⇌

[73-77] With the women on the inside, these couples now travel downstage. Starting with the inside foot they take two steps into a *grand jeté en avant* in 2nd *arabesque*; this pattern is repeated to the other side. Each woman then does a *piqué* into a high 1st *arabesque* toward her downstage corner, as the man takes a lunge toward his partner, catching her hand (her arm being outstretched backward) by reaching across his body with his left hand toward her. She then travels across to the other side of the man with two long sideward steps, the man closing into 1st position to his back foot. Both then repeat the pattern to the other side, the woman using the two steps after the *arabesque* to end in front

B1, B2, B3

[73-78] The Bolero women now move rapidly downstage performing two clockwise circles around the central couple (N and MN). They must travel a great deal on these steps, at the same time giving the other couples room for their movements. As the three of them start moving into the circle B1 must overtake B3 so as to be the leader, the others following. The step pattern resembles a turning waltz, down-up-up, but in the rhythm of 1, 2 &, 3, 4 &; performing two such waltz steps the women revolve once around themselves while continuing on the general circular line of travel. On each low traveling step the body bends diagonally toward that leg, the arm unfolding in an upward and outward curve

ner steps behind her ready for the finger turn which follows, as the woman takes a *développé croisé en avant* into a *fouetté* double turn.

N, MN

[78-80] After the finger turn the couple takes hands, right to right, left to left; then, still on *pointe*, the woman continues turning to the right, under the man's arms, raising her left arm and lowering her right in the process. The man assists her and then turns to the left under her arms, ending facing downstage left. They then let go of their left hands and the man steps to the left to be on the left side of his partner. She bends her left arm and places it so that her upper arm is resting on his right upper arm, which he braces to give her support for her balance. They end facing diagonally in toward each other, the woman having taken her right leg to *attitude*, the man having stepped backward into a lunge.

of the man. Both couples then in unison perform a *soutenu* turn *en dedans* toward the inner side of the stage.

C, MC; T, MT

[78-80] Facing the audience, the couples still moving symmetrically, the man lifts the woman in a high *entrechat six,* the woman starting with the inside foot in front, and using a full *port de bras.* Landing on [79], she springs into *relevé* on *pointe*, arms in 5th. Turning to face inward (toward downstage left for C) the woman falls sideward right in one piece, still on *pointe,* to be caught by her partner, his outside arm around her waist as he lunges to the corner. The woman brings her left arm low across her body, as she and her partner look at each other. T and MT take the symmetrical pose to C and MC.

in the same line as the upper body. This waltz pattern is repeated a total of six times.

B1, B2, B3

[79-80] Having completed their circling around N and MN, the Bolero women run during [79] to their ending places. B1 runs for only two counts; then, facing downstage right and with a *port de bras* to 5th, she performs a *pas de chat* to the right which takes her into a position in front of N and MN. On [80] she lunges across on her left leg, lowering to her right knee, and with torso tilted right diagonally forward, her arms sideward middle, slightly rounded with palms up, she looks upward diagonally to the left. B2 ends on her left leg facing downstage left, her right leg slightly bent *pointe tendue croisée,* her chest twisted to the right, both hands on her right hip, and her head up looking at the audience. B3 takes the same position to the other side.

Thus the excitement which built steadily during this active Finale concludes with a symmetrically organised stage grouping.

Curtain Calls

The following is a suggested sequence for the bows:

When the curtain comes down all leave the stage. In the order of performance of their sections in the ballet, each couple runs on, takes a low bow and retires near a chaise. The Bolero trio comes in last, retiring to center stage.

All then come forward in line and bow, after which all move backward.

Then, in turn, C, MC run forward, bow and return, then T, MT, then N, MN, and lastly the Bolero trio.

All move forward as a line, bow and retire.

Rochelle Zide Booth recalls a different arrangement:
*"For the Joffrey ballet, Tudor began with a 'picture call', the Neapolitan girl coming off **pointe** to **tendue** back, the arms remaining the same as in the attitude balance at the end of the ballet.*

In the blackout (or curtain down) we cleared the stage and began the bows as above, only we did them in order, ending with the Neapolitan instead of the Bolero. I like yours better, and it is possible we did it with the Neapolitan last because Jerry Arpino danced the Neapolitan."

LABANOTATION GLOSSARY

Arms

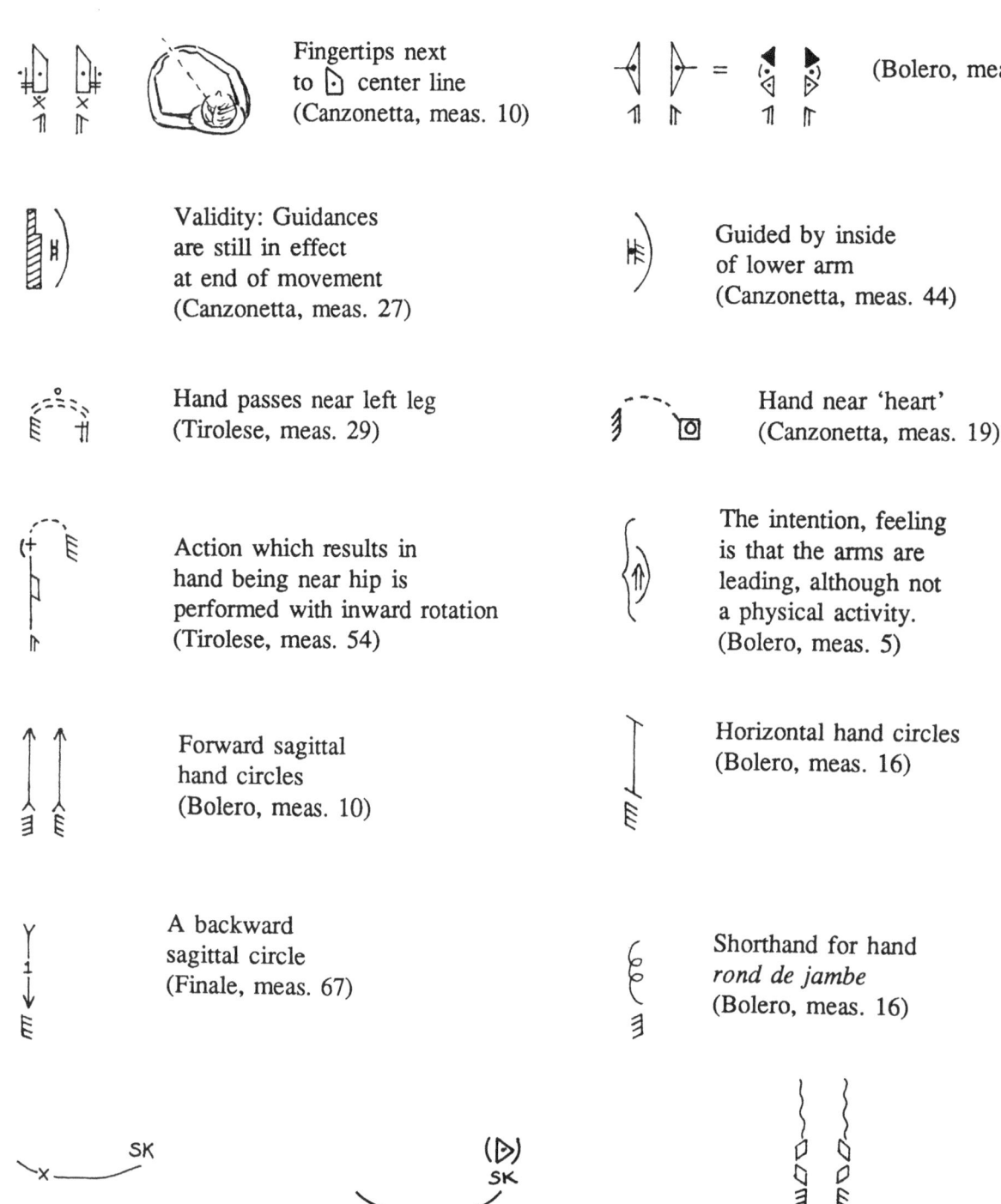

Legs

'Run' = quick steps, i.e., get there fast (Canzonetta, meas. 12)

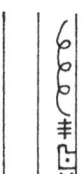

Shorthand for small triple *ronds de jambe en dehors* for lower leg called *'jouer'* (Canzonetta, meas. 4)

Amalgamated turn (Bolero, meas. 14)

Timing

Free duration of movements within the time frame (Canzonetta, meas. 44)

Fermata (Tirolese, meas. 10)

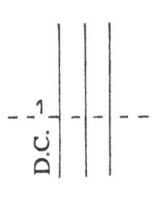

D.C. = Dancer's Counts indicated only on page 42, otherwise understood. An extended dotted line shows the start of a new 'dancer's counts' phrase. (Opening March, meas. 1)

Without a duration line this is not a sudden movement; it occurs without timing awareness. (Opening March, meas. 9)

Dynamics

Unemphasised (Opening March, meas. 10)

Hands relaxed (Opening March, meas. 80)

Emphasised (stressed) (Canzonetta, meas. 16)

Eyes strong, piercing (Bolero, starting position)

Press forward and upward (Tirolese, meas. 64)

Floor Plans

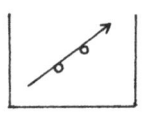 Direction, number and location of turns on a straight path (Tirolese, meas. 27-32)

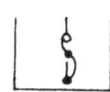 Holding hands - the small black dot represents the hands (Opening March, meas. 43)

 Two people (Canzonetta, meas. 1-2)

 More than two people (Bolero, meas. 43)

Repeats

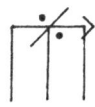 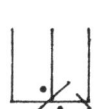 Repeat centered at end of staff is shown to be the same for the reminder at the start of the next staff (Tirolese, meas. 43-44)

 Placed at the left of score: Only footwork of meas. 48 is written here, all other details to be added as in meas. 48 (Canzonetta, meas. 50)

 Only footwork for repeat to the other side is written; all other details to be added (Opening March, meas. 59)

 This measure (material) repeated 4 times (Tirolese, meas. 82)

 This material repeated 4 times alternating sides (Bolero, meas. 35)

Analogy Sign

MT ≕ MT performs lateral symmetry of others (Opening March, before meas. 57)

Miscellaneous

 Women   ♀s Men   P Partner   ∧ Cancellation: no longer in effect (Canzonetta, meas. 30)

 No longer having a designated focus (Opening March, meas. 16)

 Look away from partner (Canzonetta, meas. 15)

LABANOTATION GLOSSARY

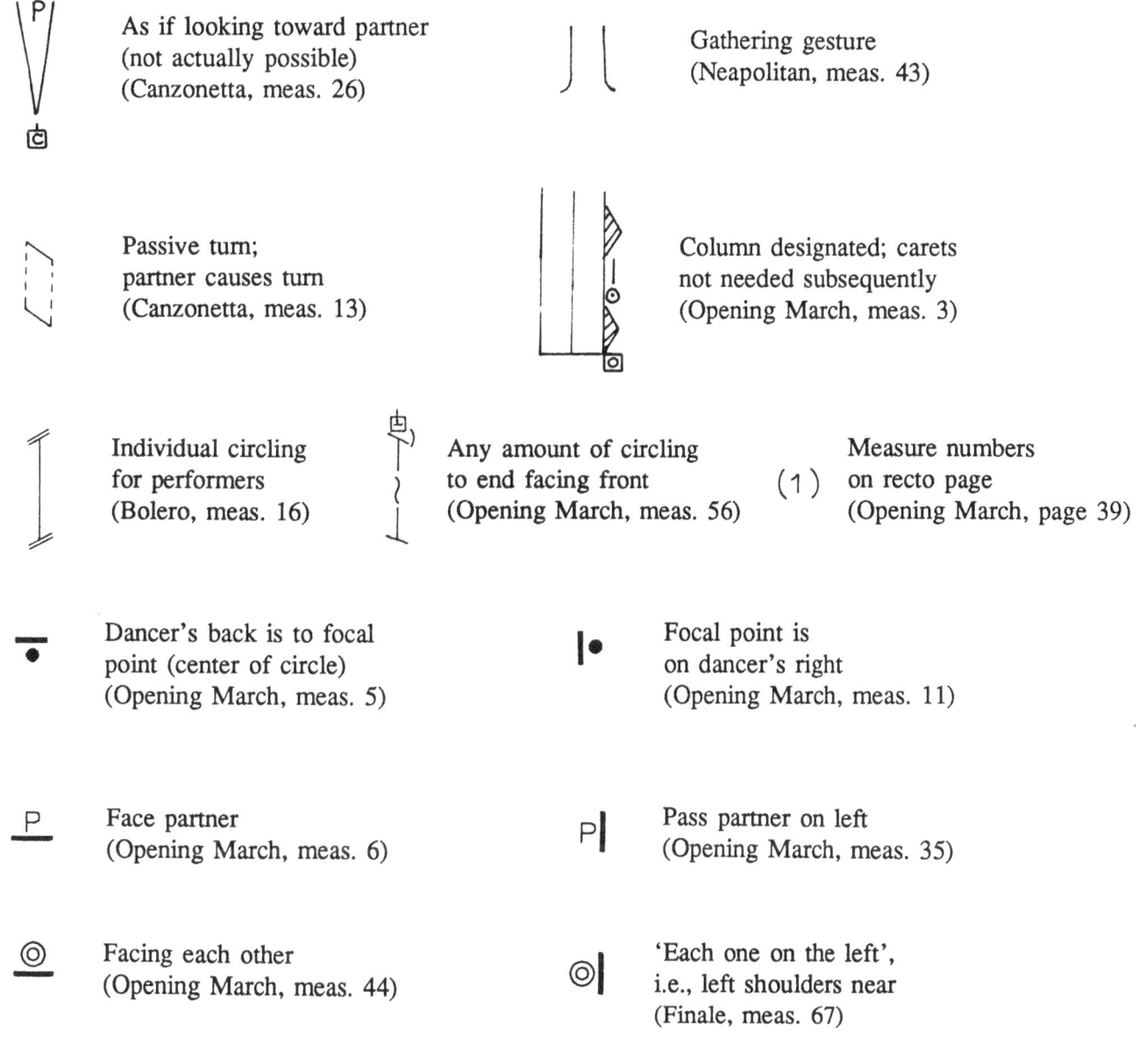

	As if looking toward partner (not actually possible) (Canzonetta, meas. 26)		Gathering gesture (Neapolitan, meas. 43)
	Passive turn; partner causes turn (Canzonetta, meas. 13)		Column designated; carets not needed subsequently (Opening March, meas. 3)
	Individual circling for performers (Bolero, meas. 16)	Any amount of circling to end facing front (Opening March, meas. 56)	Measure numbers on recto page (Opening March, page 39)
	Dancer's back is to focal point (center of circle) (Opening March, meas. 5)		Focal point is on dancer's right (Opening March, meas. 11)
	Face partner (Opening March, meas. 6)		Pass partner on left (Opening March, meas. 35)
	Facing each other (Opening March, meas. 44)		'Each one on the left', i.e., left shoulders near (Finale, meas. 67)

TERMINOLOGY

'Glissade-like step', 'sketchy *glissade*' = quick, not fully articulated.

Piqué = a step on *pointe*.

Relevé = a rise. Sprung *relevé* = a snatched *relevé*, the weight lifted slightly off the floor.

Run = quick traveling steps, not actually airborne.

For Arm Positions: *Bras bas*   1st position   'Arms 5th overhead'

THE THREE GRACES

| Marie Taglioni | Fanny Elssler | Carlotta Grisi |
| *La Sylphide* | *Cachucha* | *Pas de Diane* |

This illustration shows the centre group's opening pose.

THE CHOREOGRAPHIC SCORE

OF

SOIREE MUSICALE

OPENING MARCH

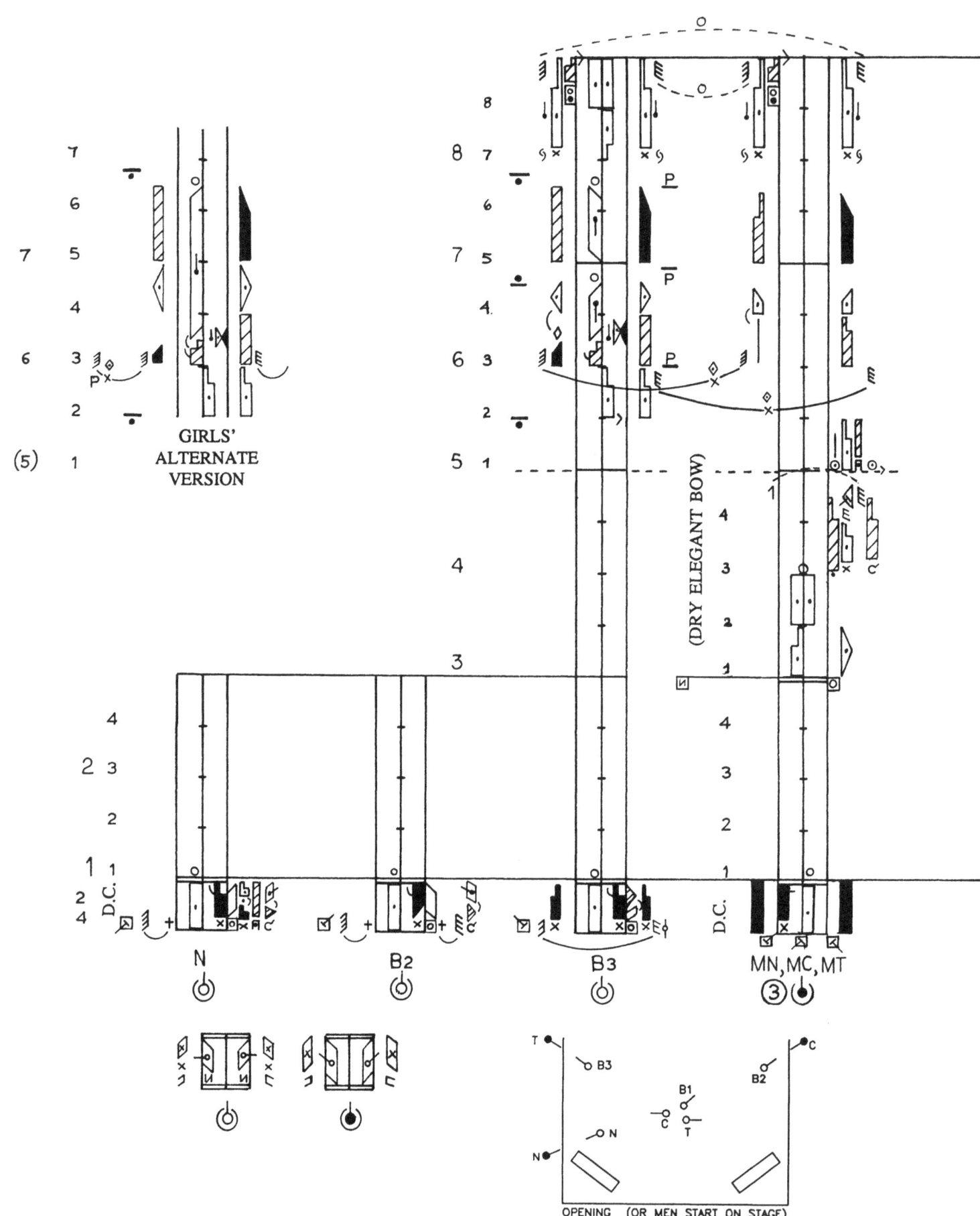

OPENING MARCH

Meas. 8 & 9
The Scottish Theatre Ballet.
Couples in the 'Oval Circle' pose.
Dancers (L to R): Bruce Steivel, Amanda Olivier,
Patricia Rianne, Anne Allan, Elaine McDonald, Hilary Debden,
Michael Beare, Sally Collard-Gentle, Harold King.

(Anthony Crickmay)

44 SOIREE MUSICALE

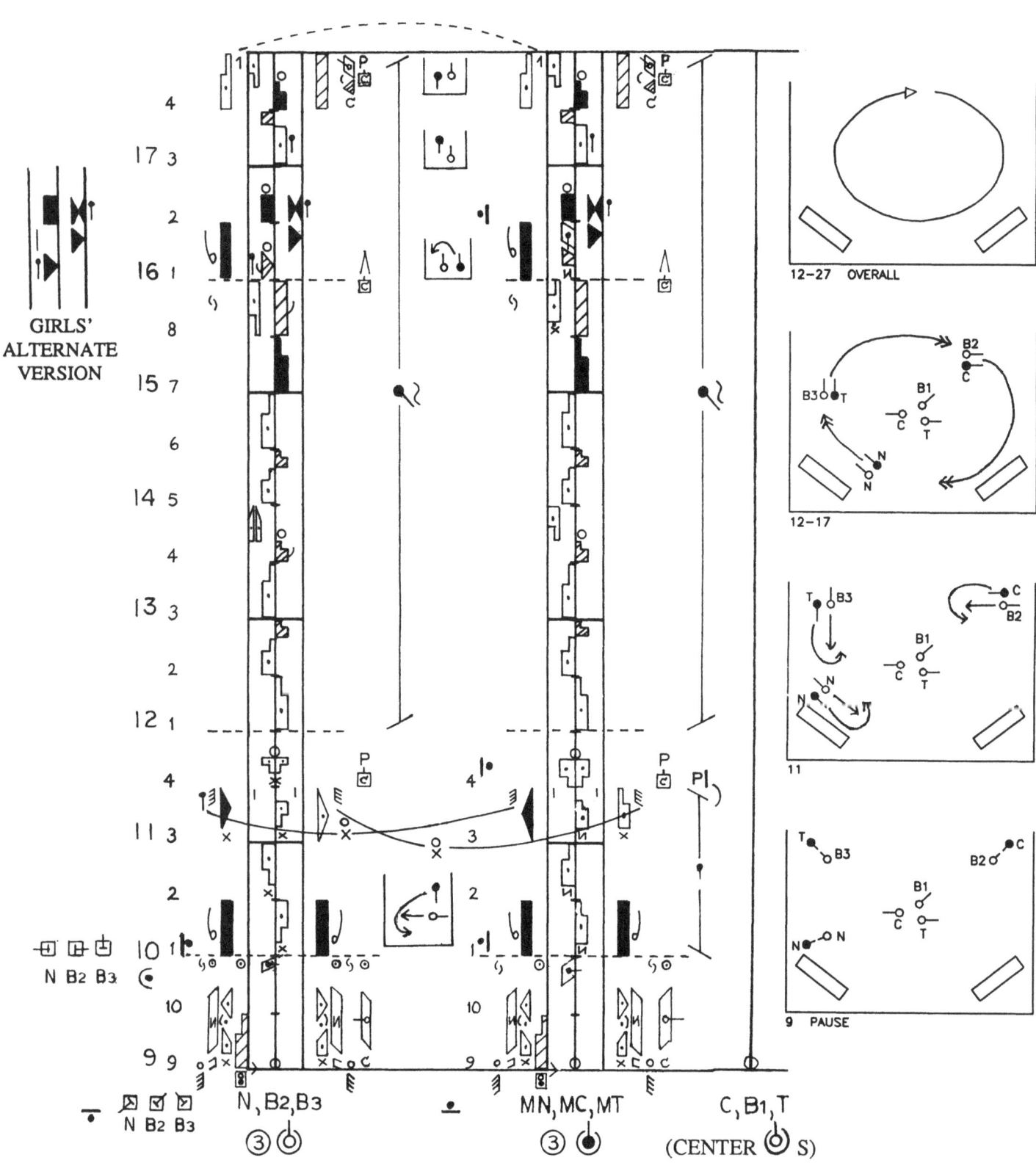

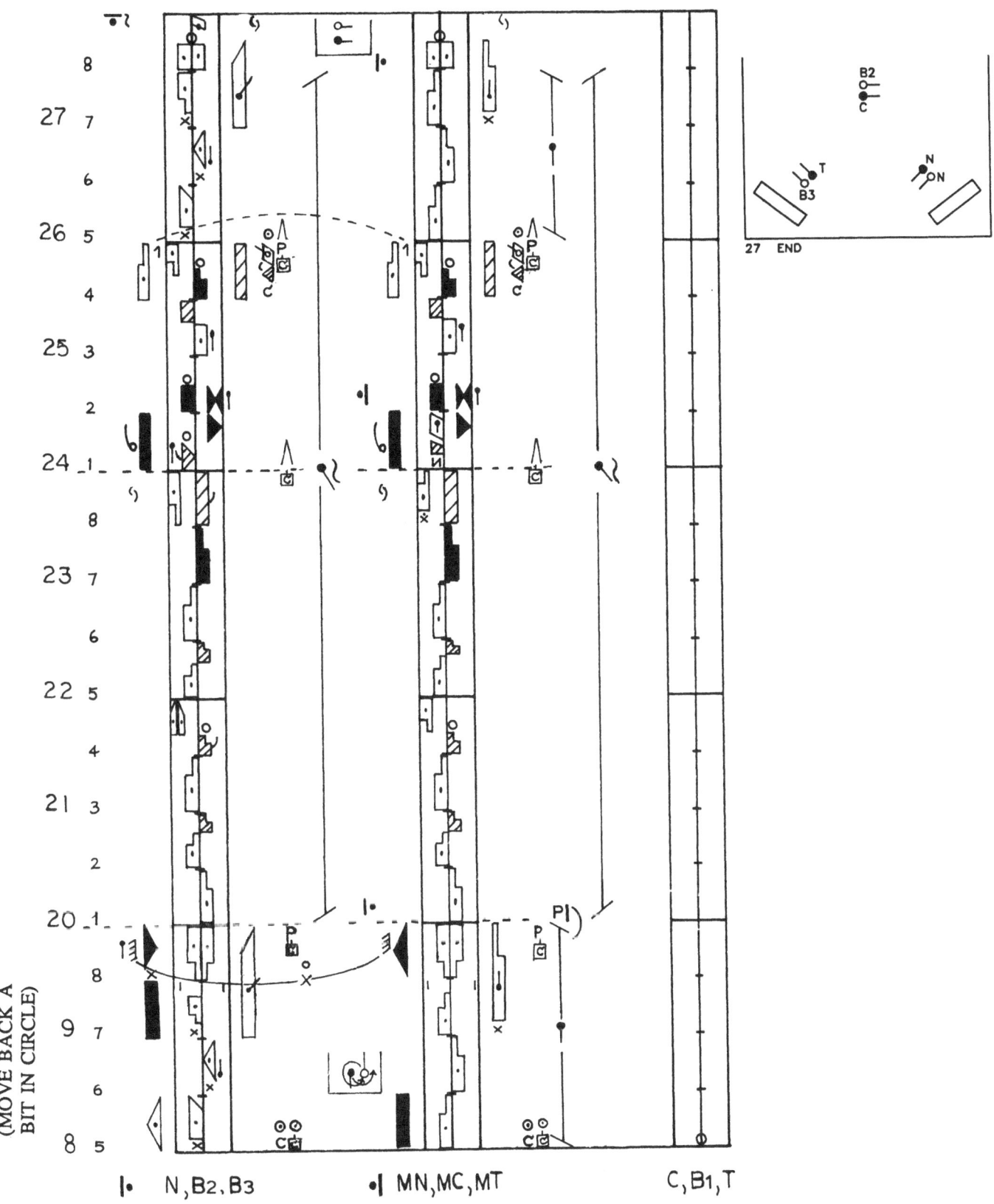

Meas. 29-30
London Ballet in *Soirée Musicale* at the Toynbee Hall, London 1938-39.
The *relevé* in *attitude* after the long low *chassé*.
Dancers (L to R): Gerd Larsen, Guy Massey, Monica Boam,
Charlotte Bidmead, Rosa Vernon (back to camera), Peggy van Praagh,
Antony Tudor, Maude Lloyd (back to camera), Hugh Laing.

(Will Rapport)

Meas. 32
The Joffrey Ballet Company.
Circling one's partner with the dainty 'limping' step. Rochelle Zide in the foreground with Paul Sutherland, Mary Ellen Jackson and Brunhilda Ruiz.

OPENING MARCH

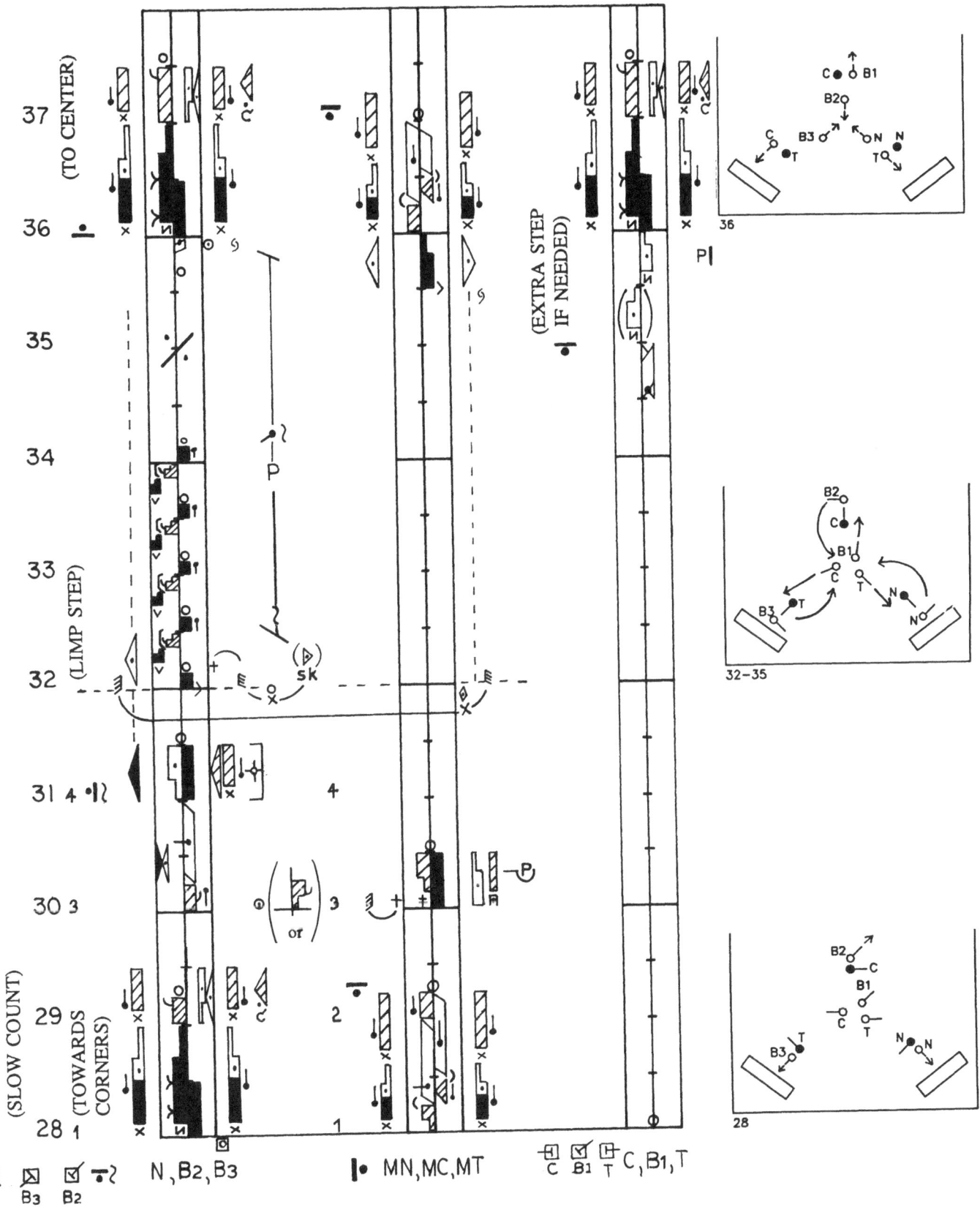

48 SOIREE MUSICALE

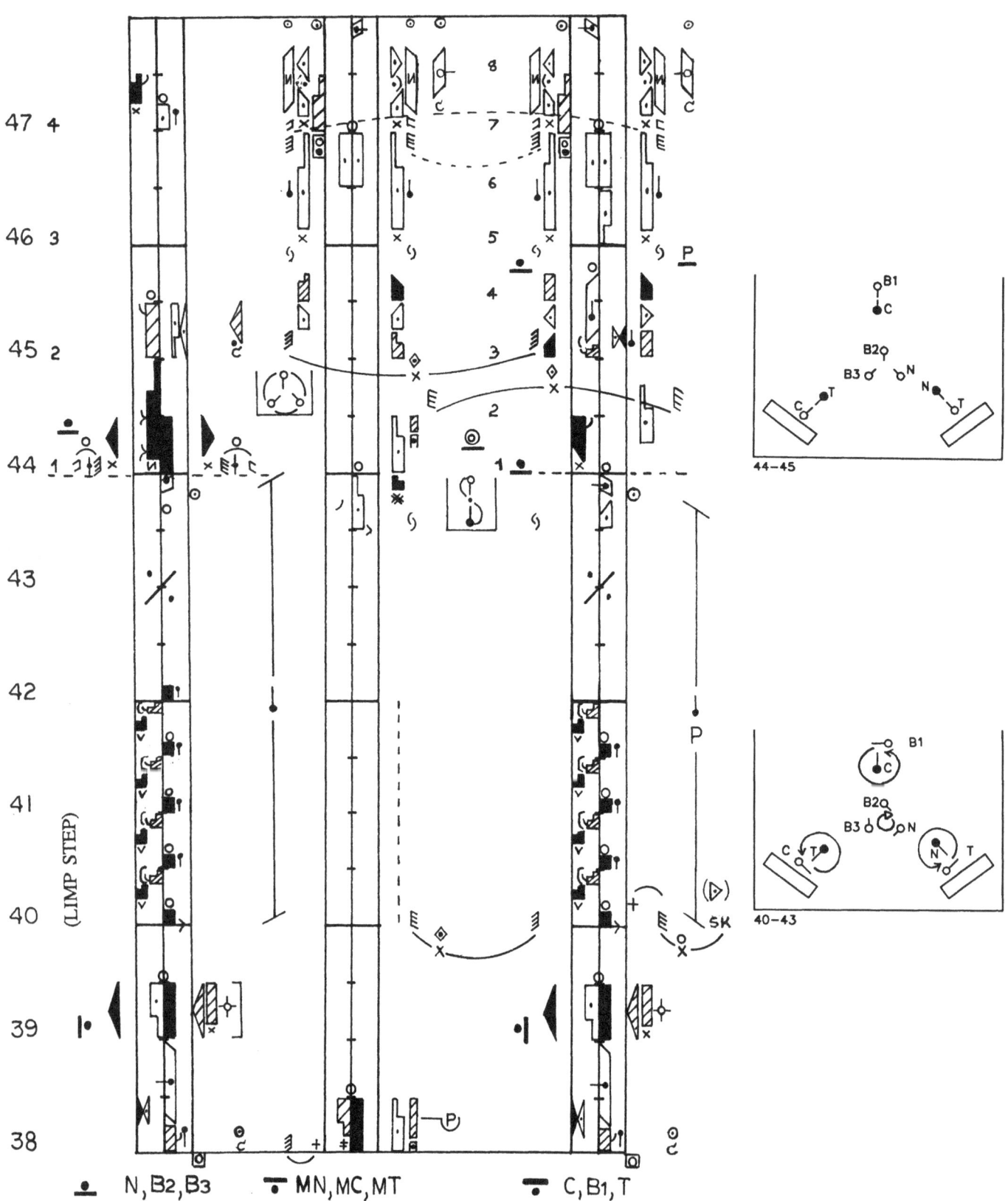

OPENING MARCH

49

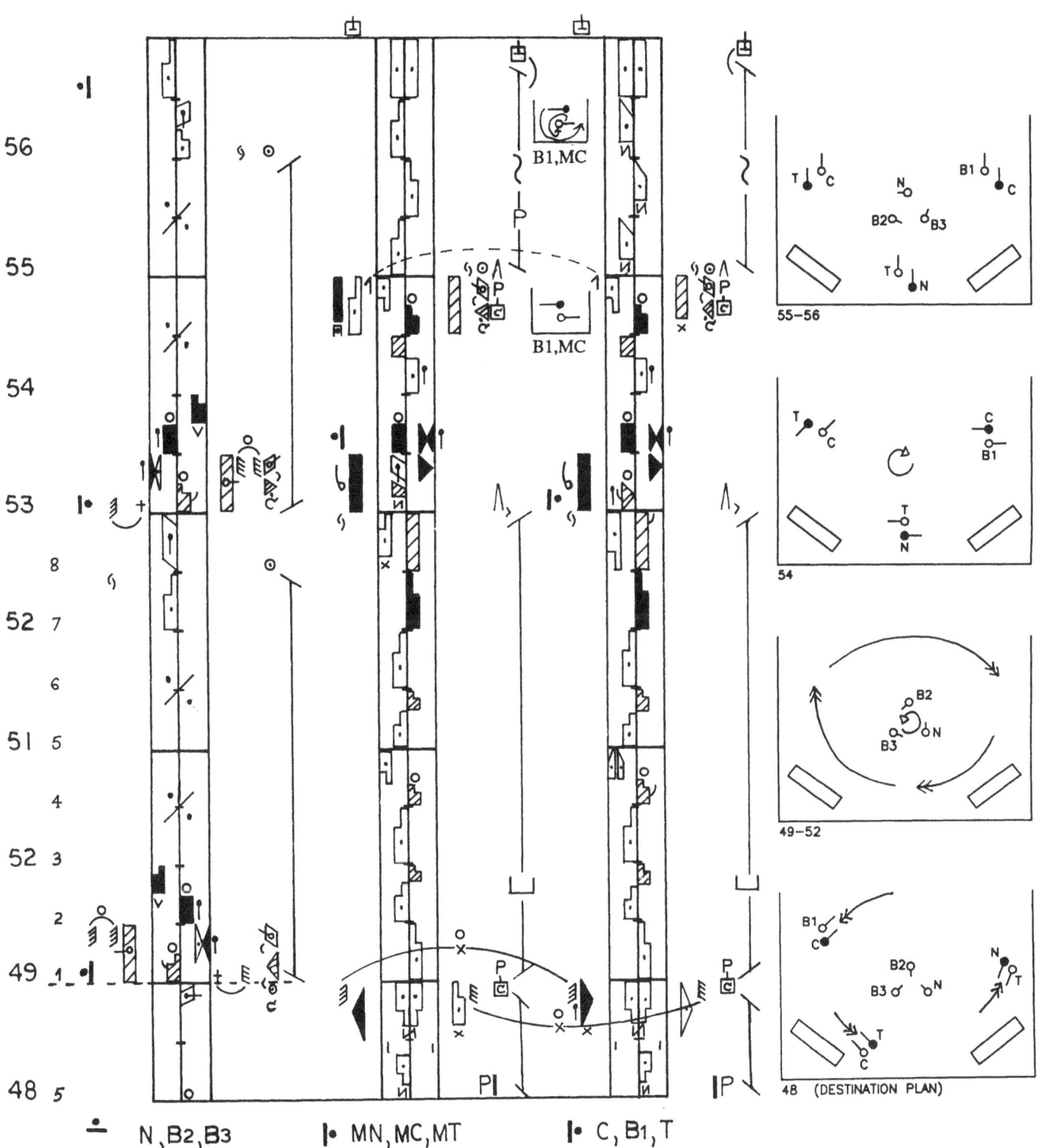

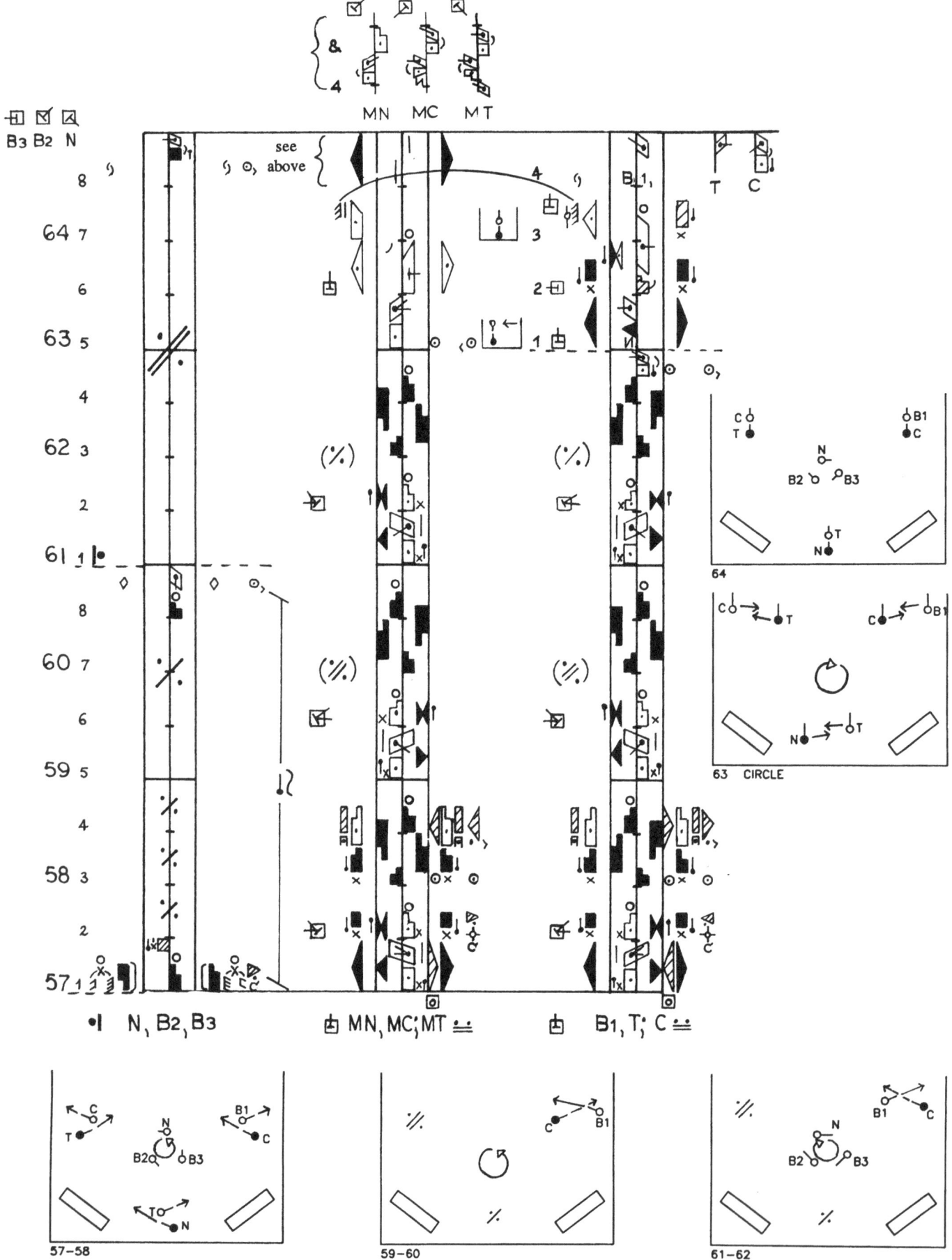

Meas. 58
The Scottish Theatre Ballet.
The couples cross with a *jeté avant*.
(Note that in the score the center women are circling, they are not in a pose as shown here.)
Dancers (L to R): Anne Allan, Anthony Parnell, Patricia Rianne, Amanda Olivier,
Hilary Debden, Sally Collard-Gentle, Michael Beare, Harold King, Elaine McDonald.

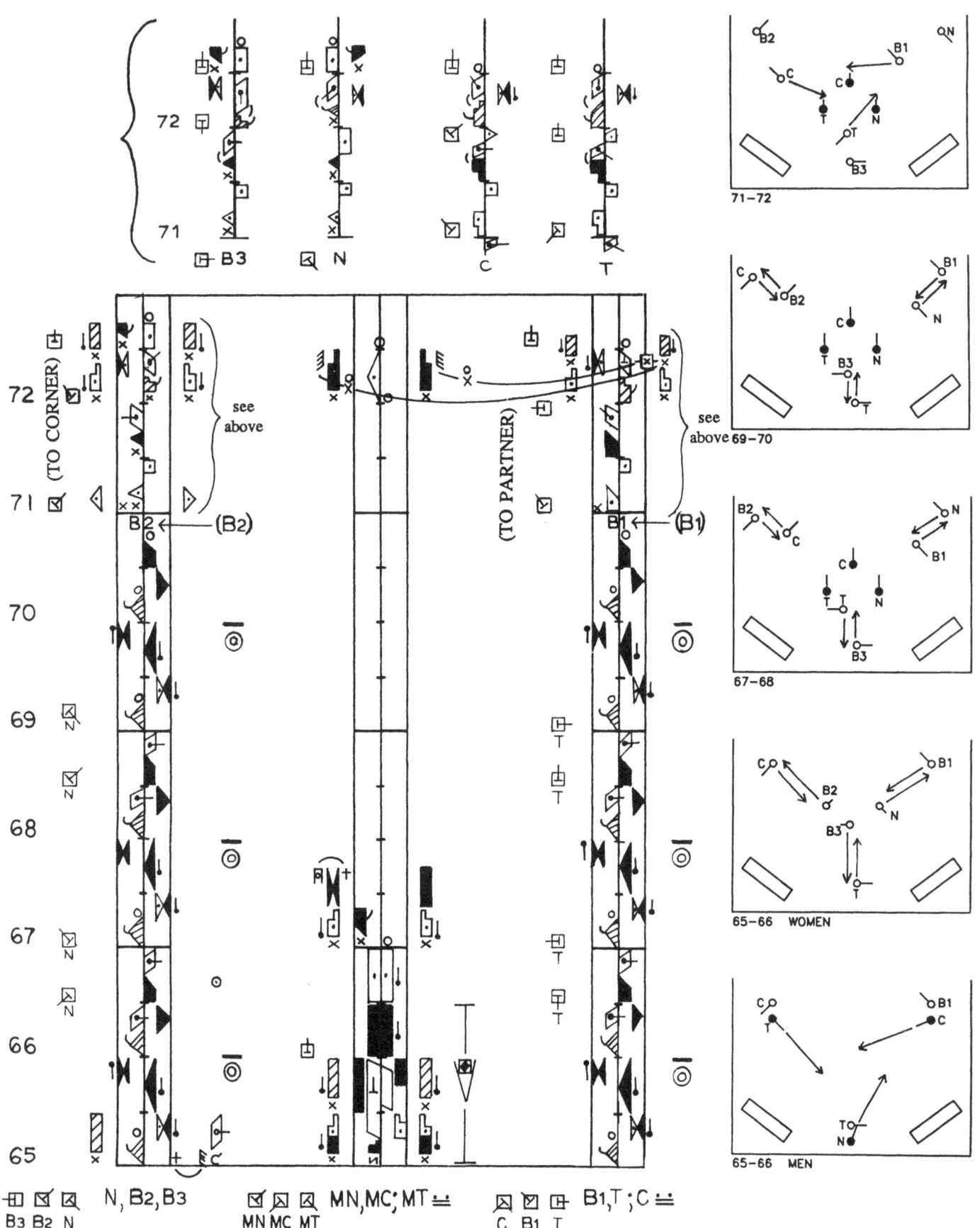

OPENING MARCH

END OF OPENING MARCH   TRANSITION TO CANZONETTA

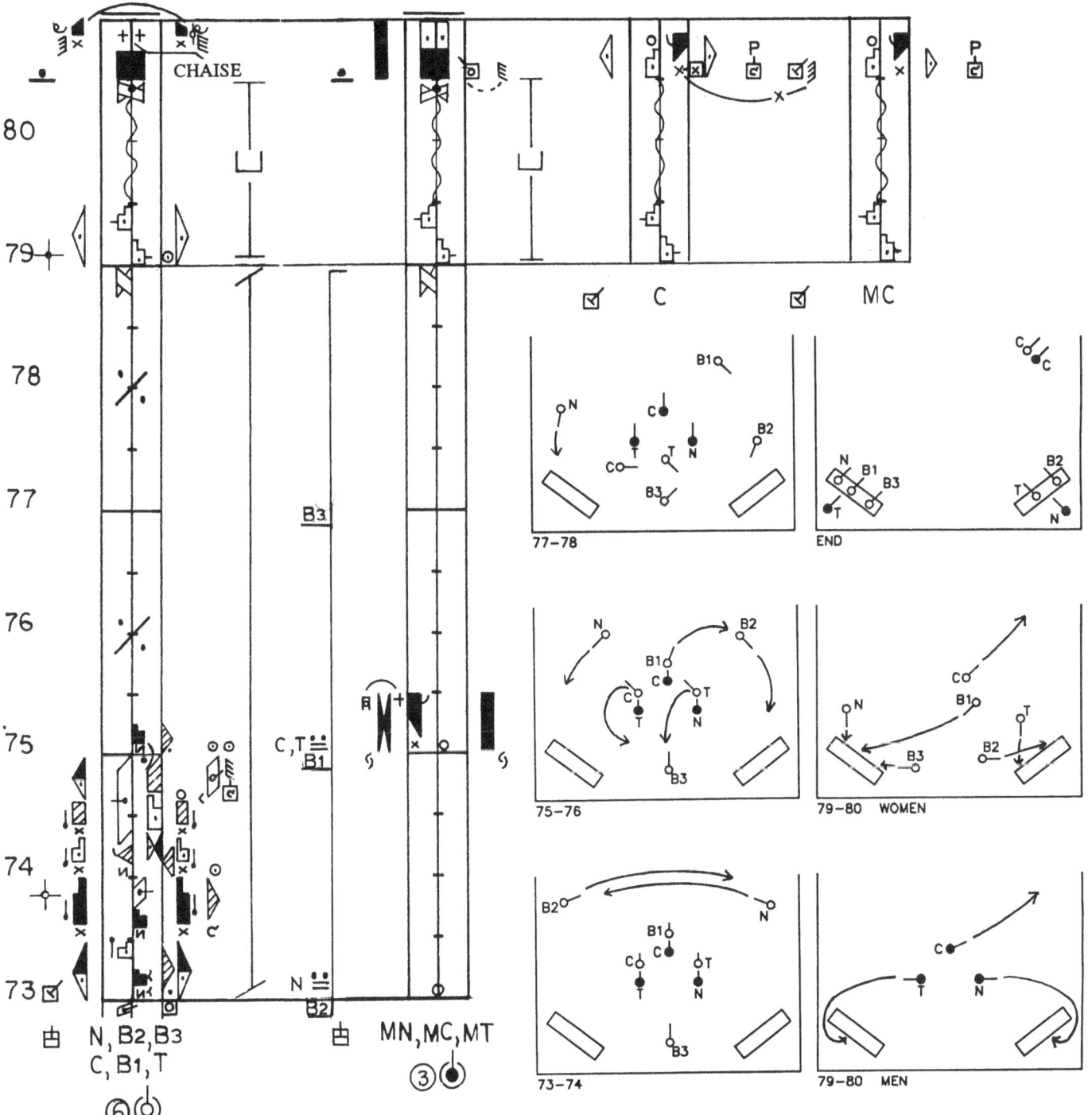

End of meas. 4
The Scottish Theatre Ballet.
Looking back, after the *jouer*. (Note that the man should be more on her left side and also lower since he looks up at her.)
Elaine Mc Donald with Anthony Parnell.

Meas. 4
The Scottish Theatre Ballet.
The *jouer* foot movement. (The body should be more forward toward the foot.)
Dancers as above.

Meas. 3
The Scottish Theatre Ballet.
Landing from the *jeté*.
Dancers as above.

CANZONETTA

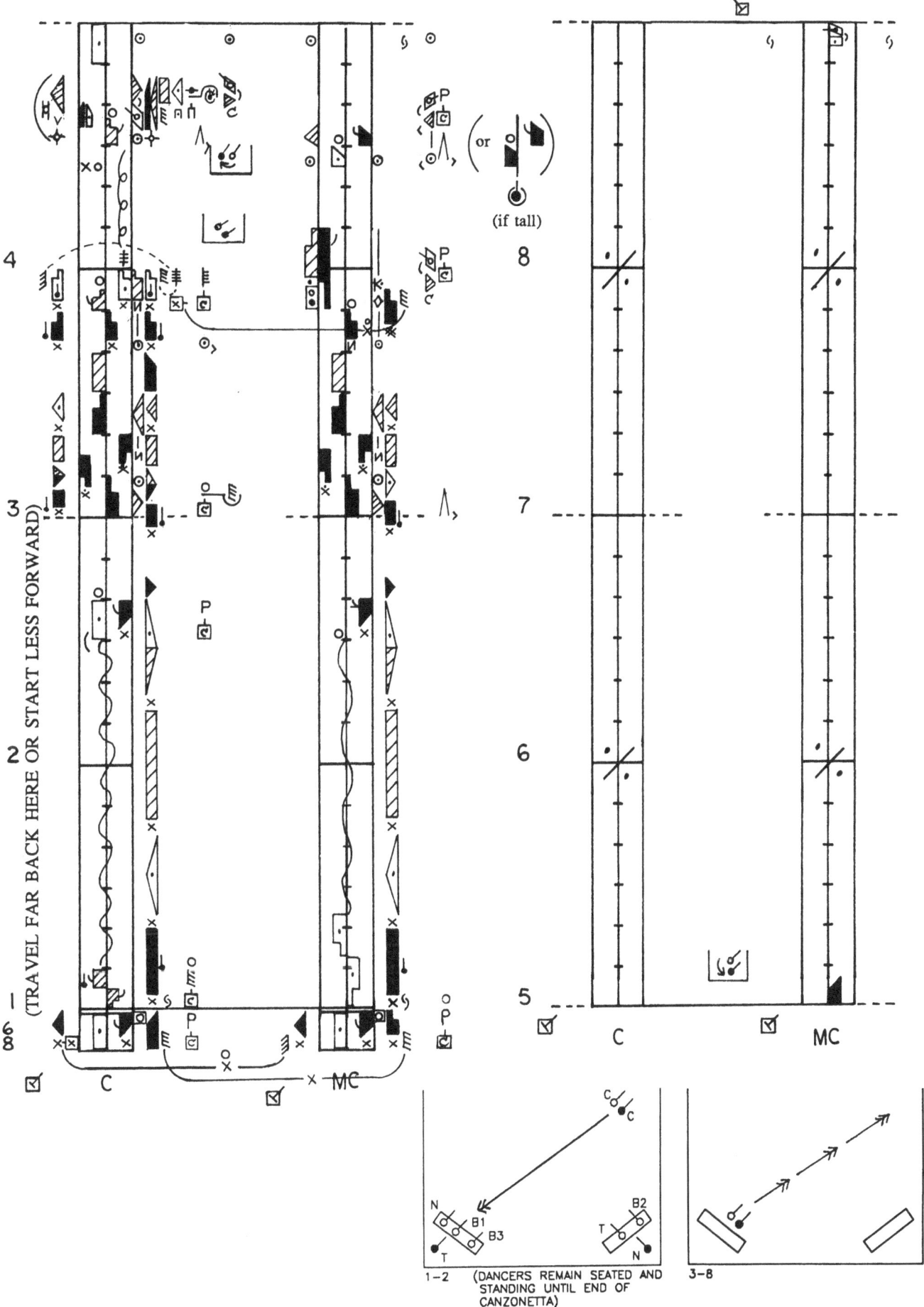

SOIREE MUSICALE

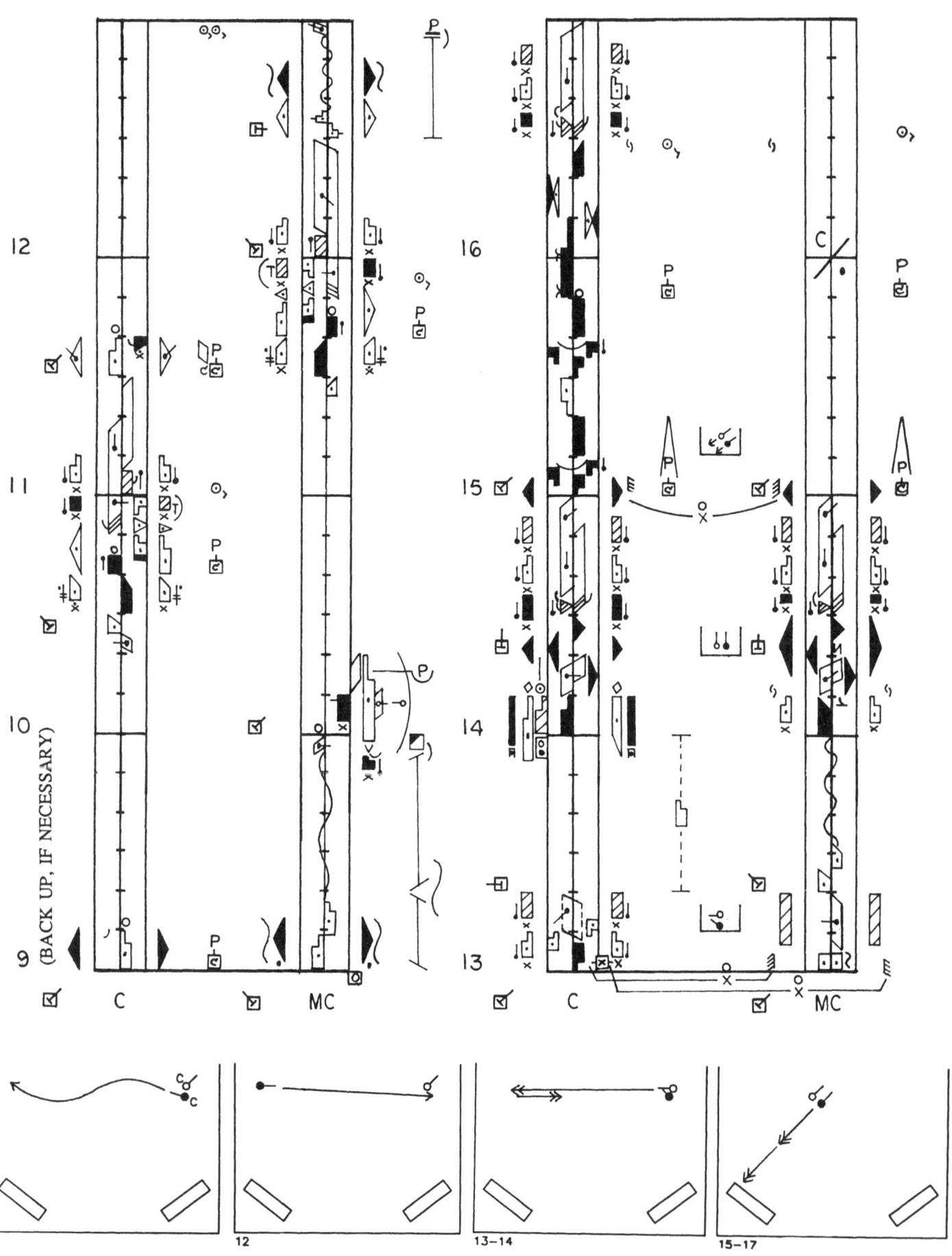

CANZONETTA

57

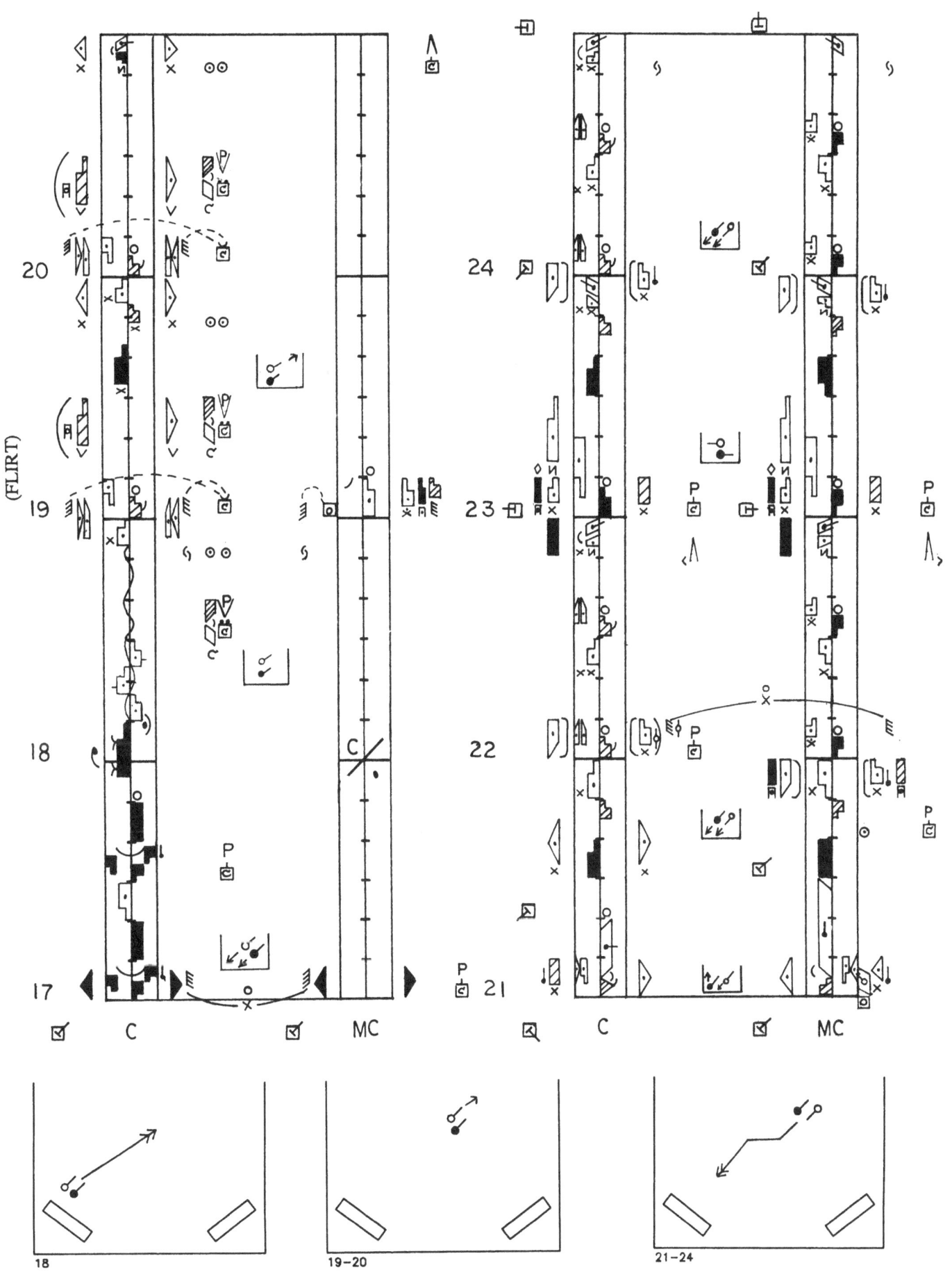

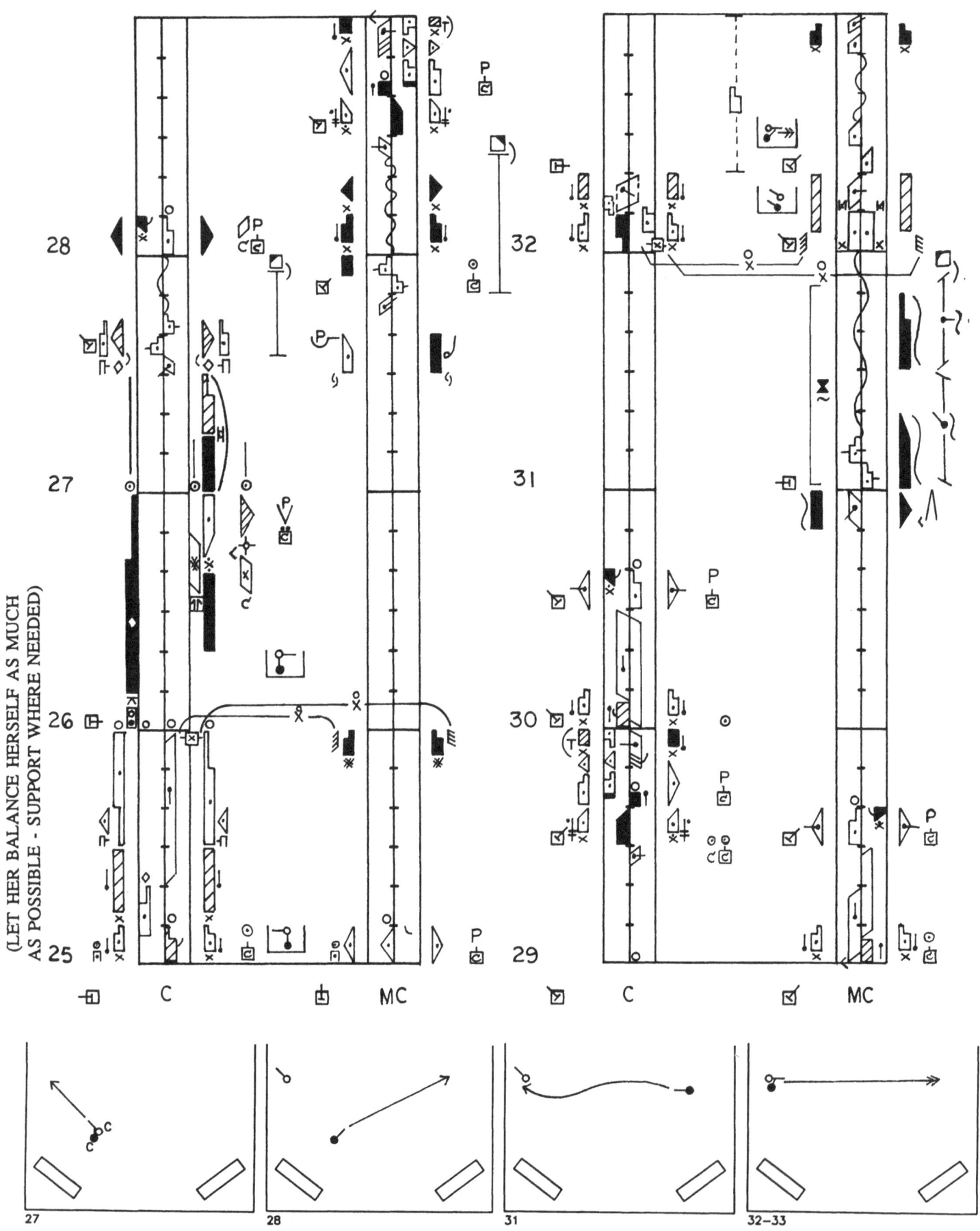

CANZONETTA

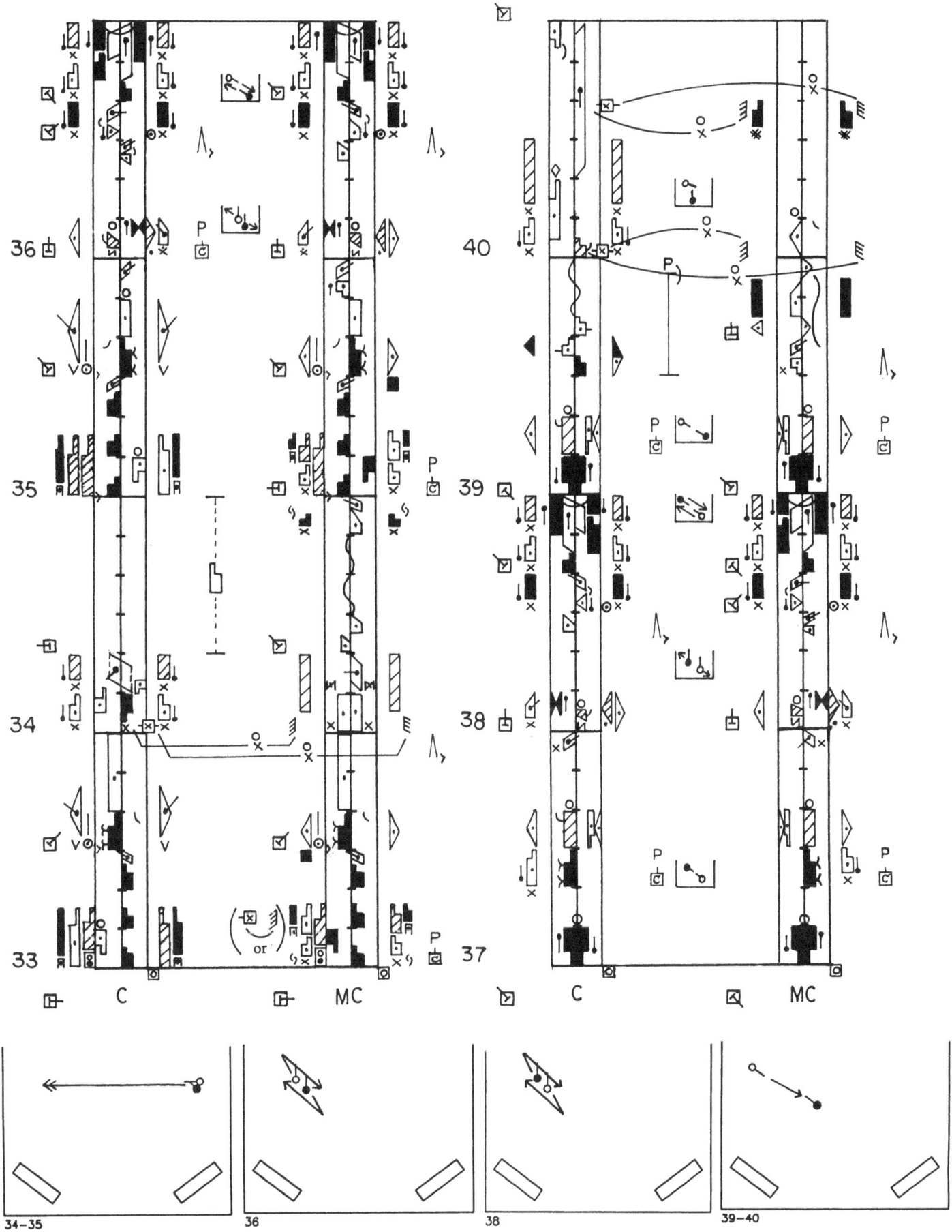

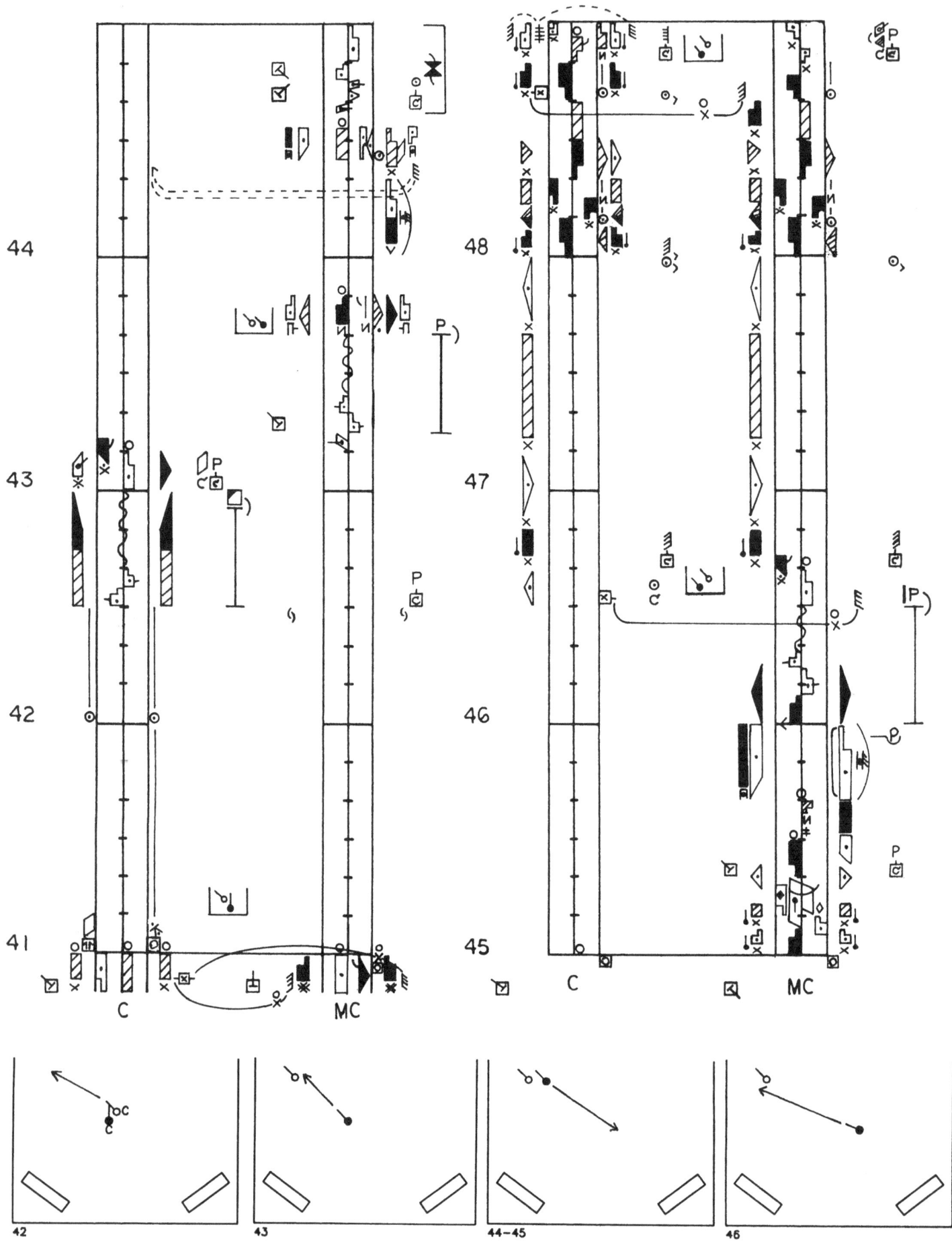

CANZONETTA

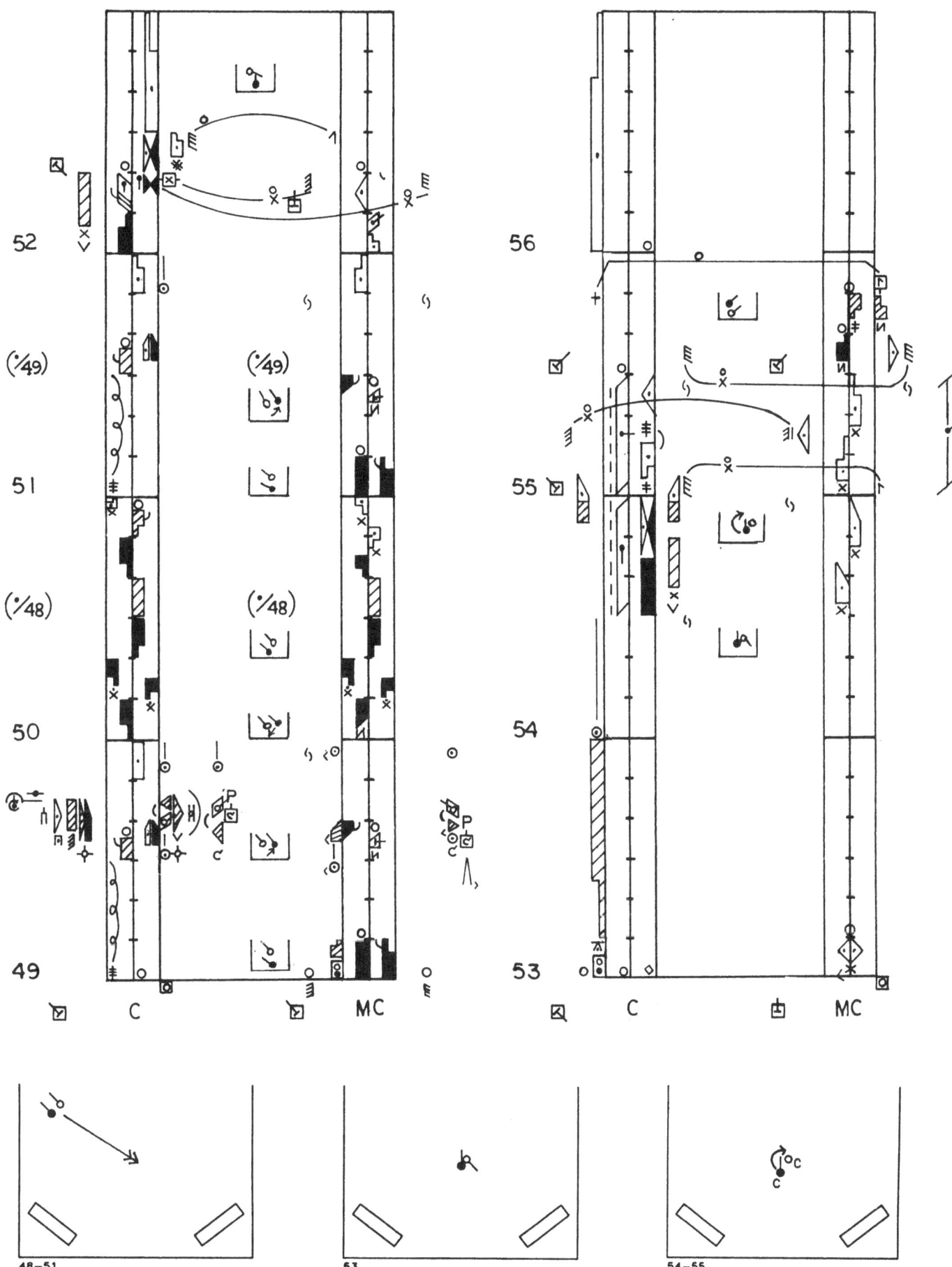

END OF CANZONETTA

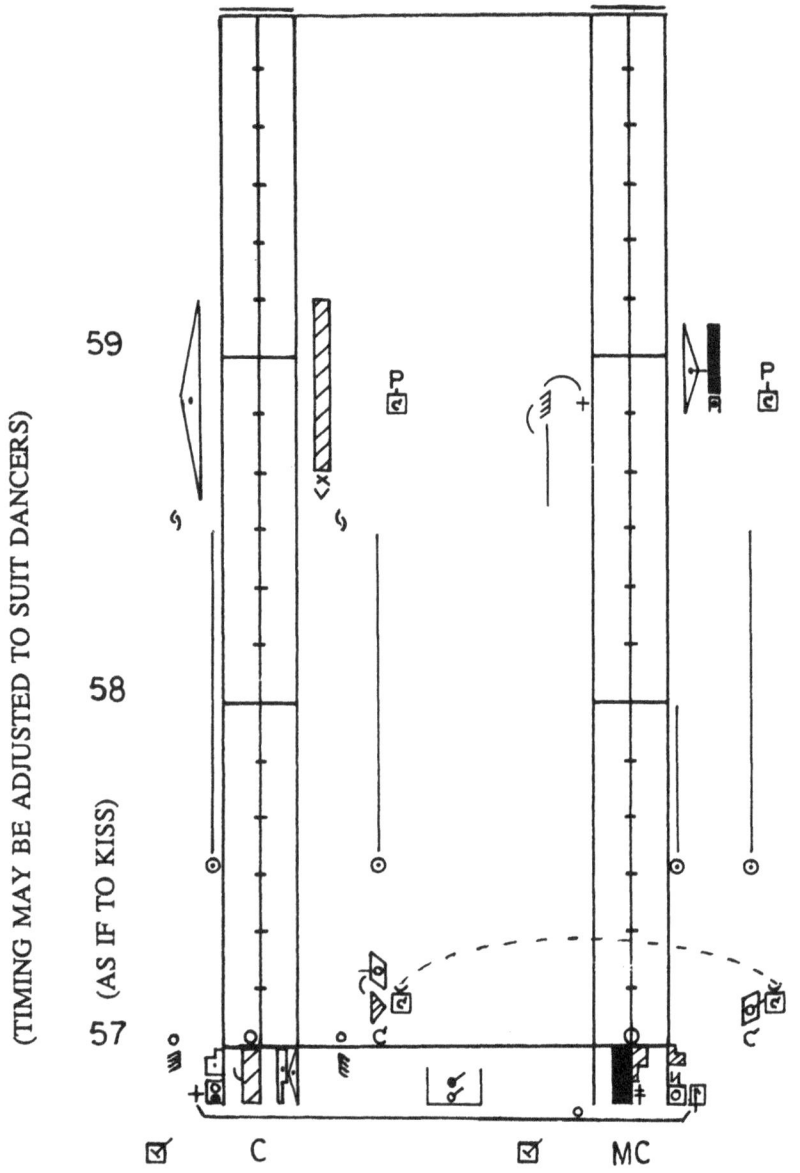
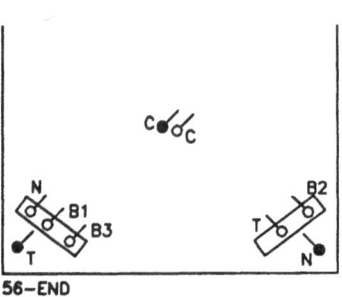
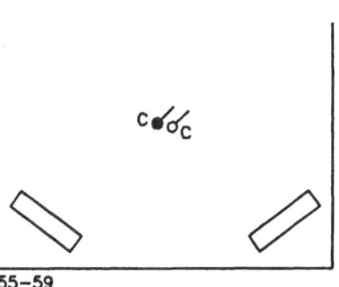

CANZONETTA

TRANSITION TO TIROLESE

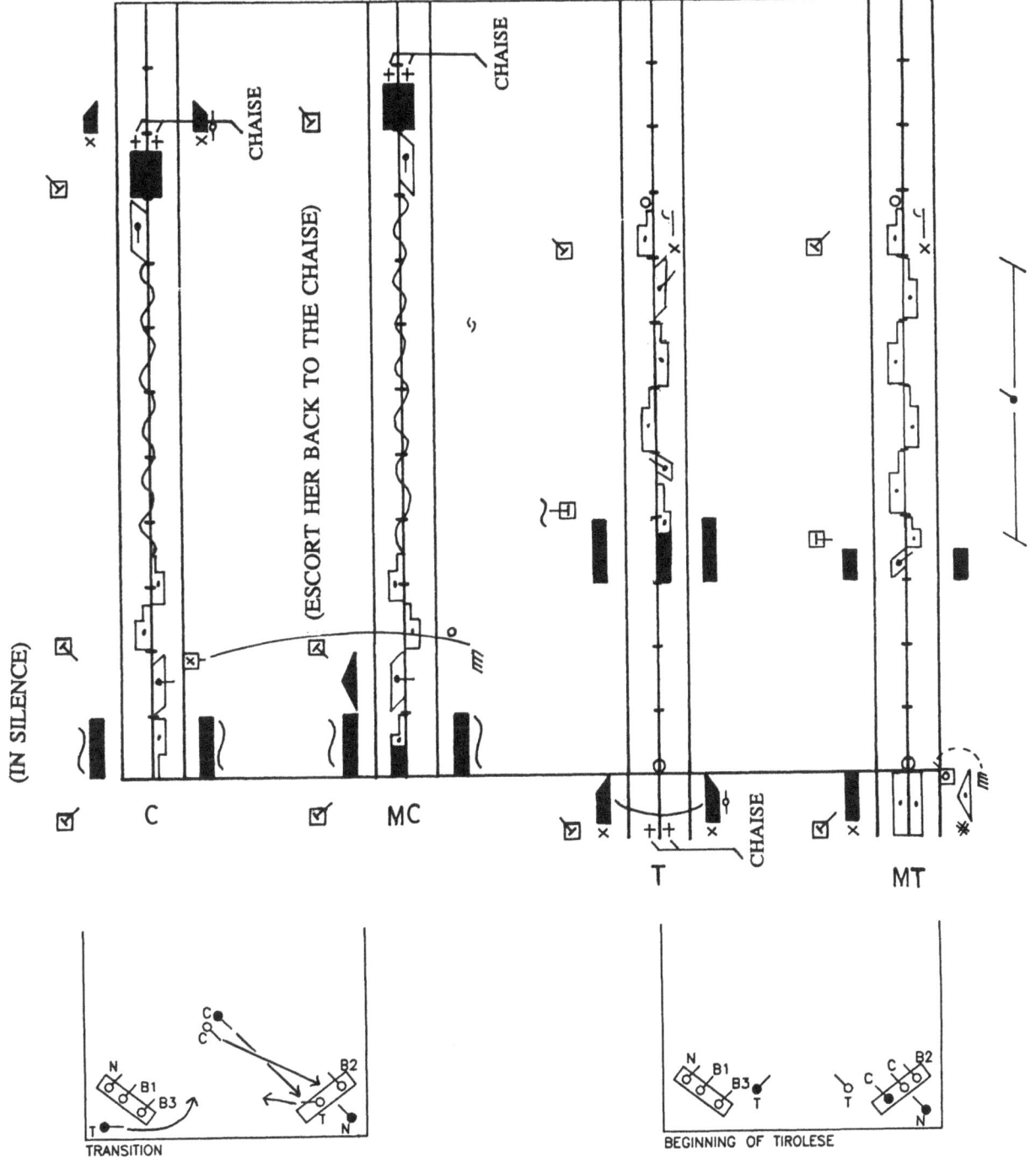

Meas. 15
The Scottish Theatre Ballet.
Pulling back (the *raccourci*) on *pointe*. Harold King dancing with Patricia Rianne in the foreground. Dancers (L to R): Amanda Olivier, Elaine McDonald, Anthony Parnell seated with Michael Beare standing behind; Sally Collard-Gentle, Hilary Debden (seated) with Anne Allan standing behind.

Meas. 36
The Scottish Theatre Ballet.
The high extension which follows the *arabesque* balancing on the man's arm, facing upstage left.
Dancers as above.

Meas. 102
The Scottish Theatre Ballet.
The front *attitude* toward each other, first performed at a lower level (meas. 6) but more exaggerated in the repeat.
Dancers as above.

TIROLESE

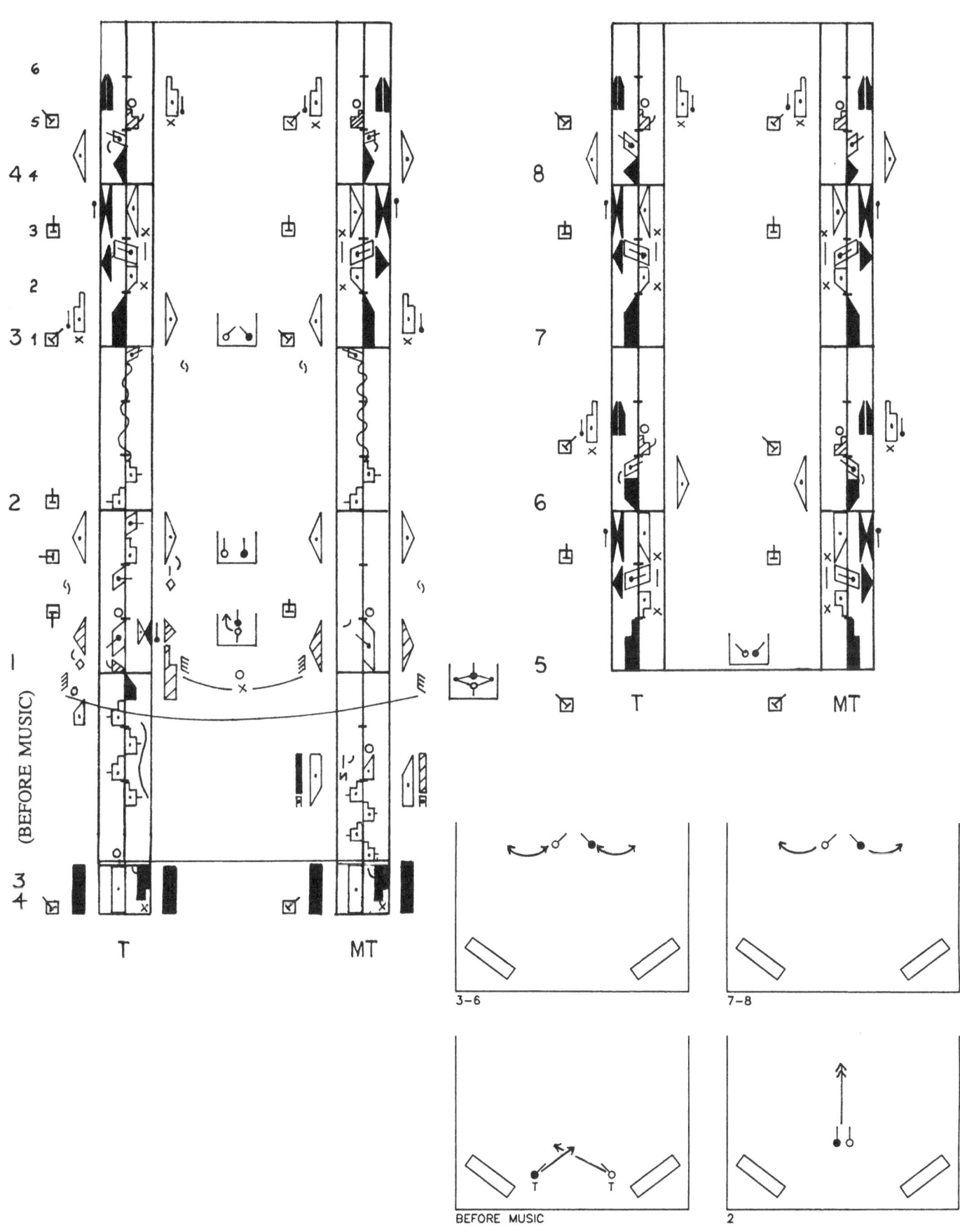

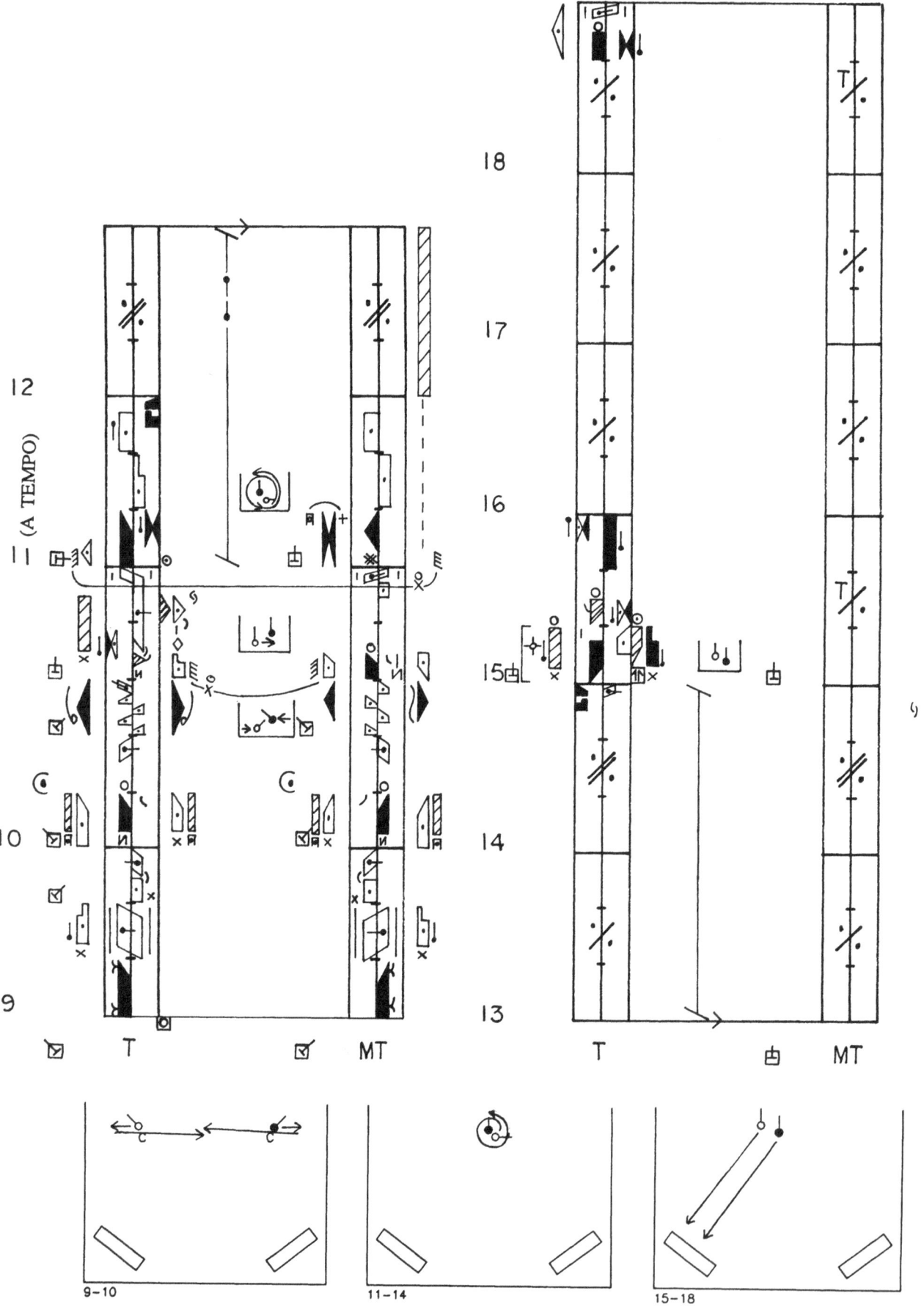

TIROLESE

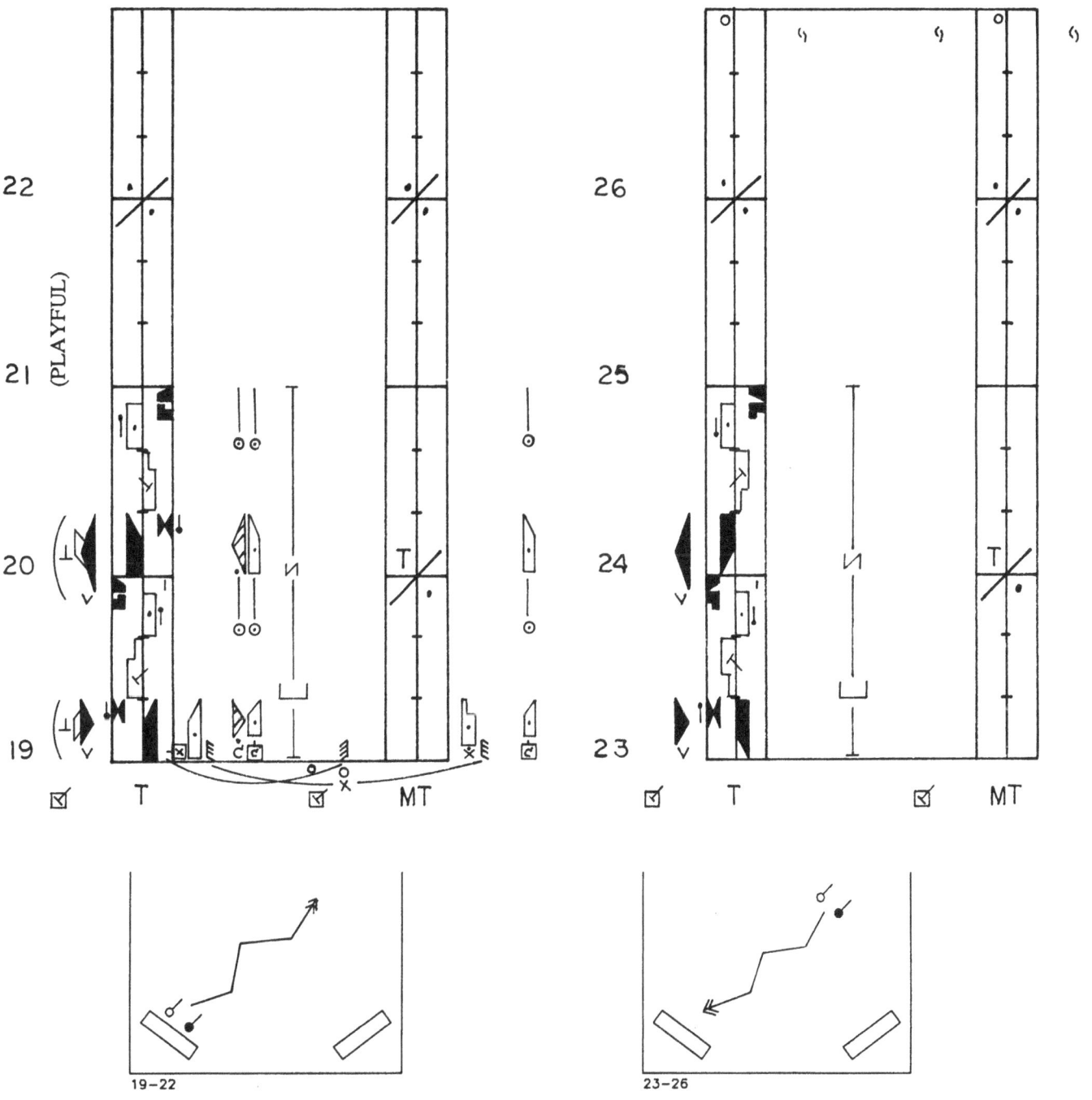

68   SOIREE MUSICALE

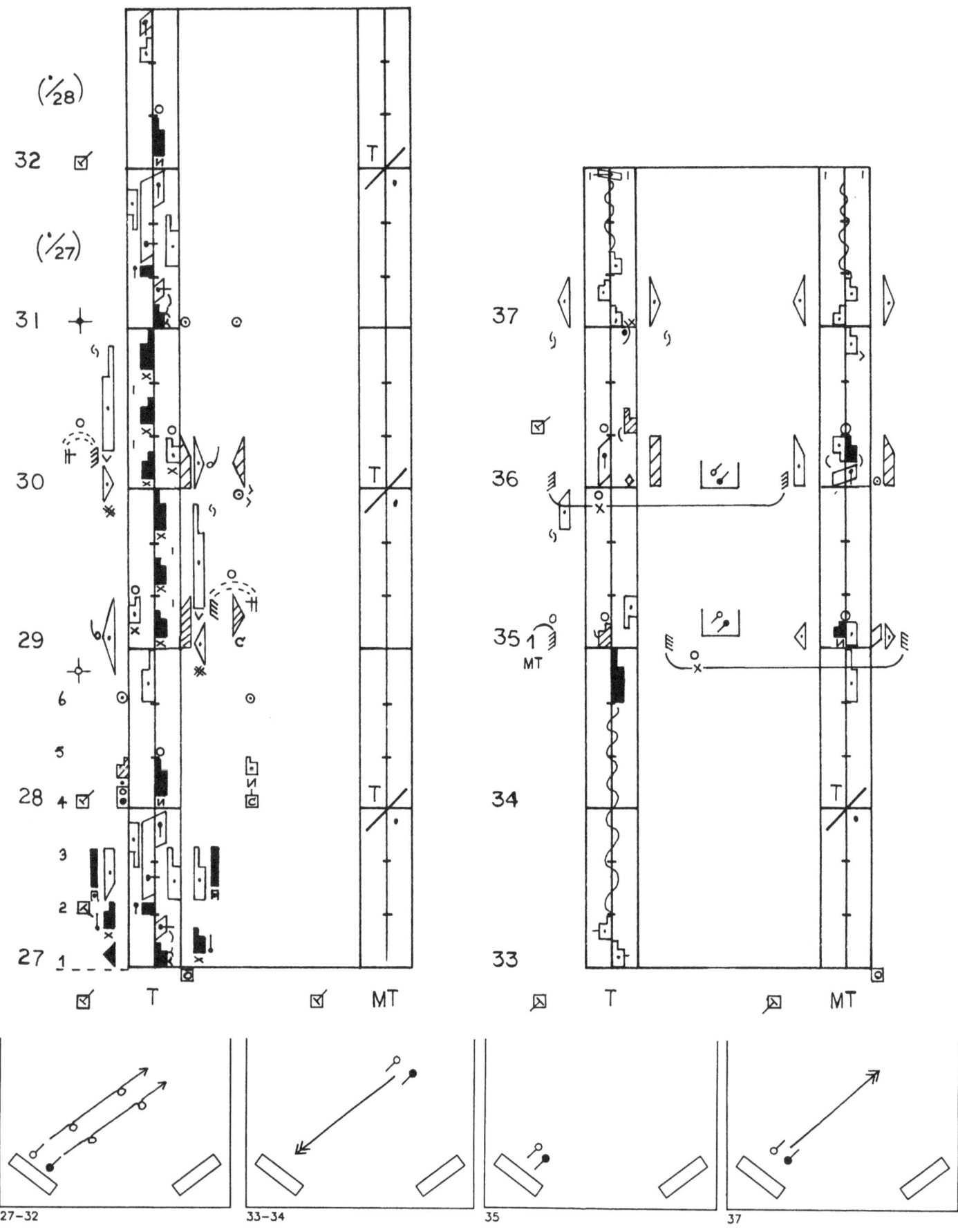

TIROLESE

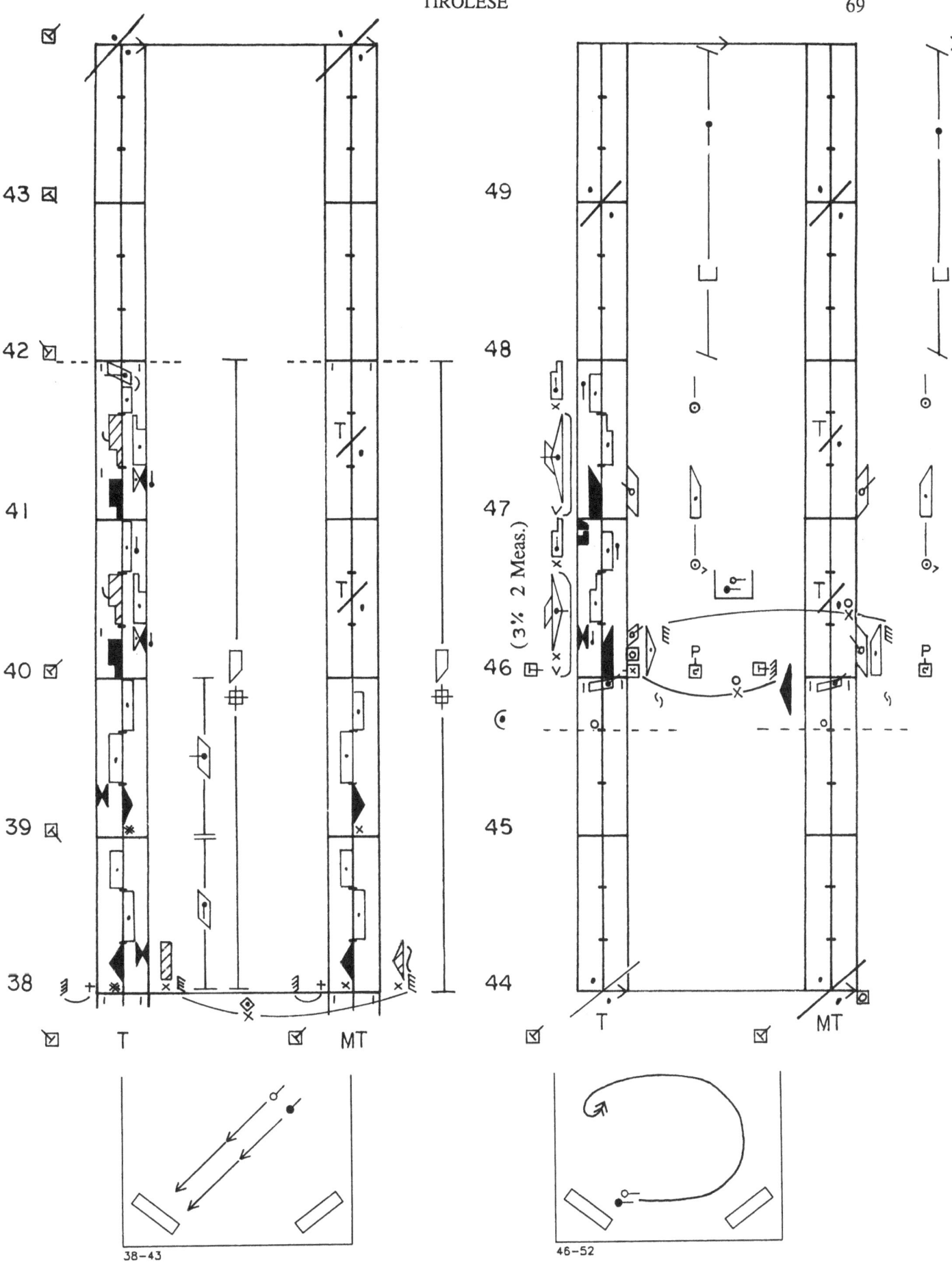

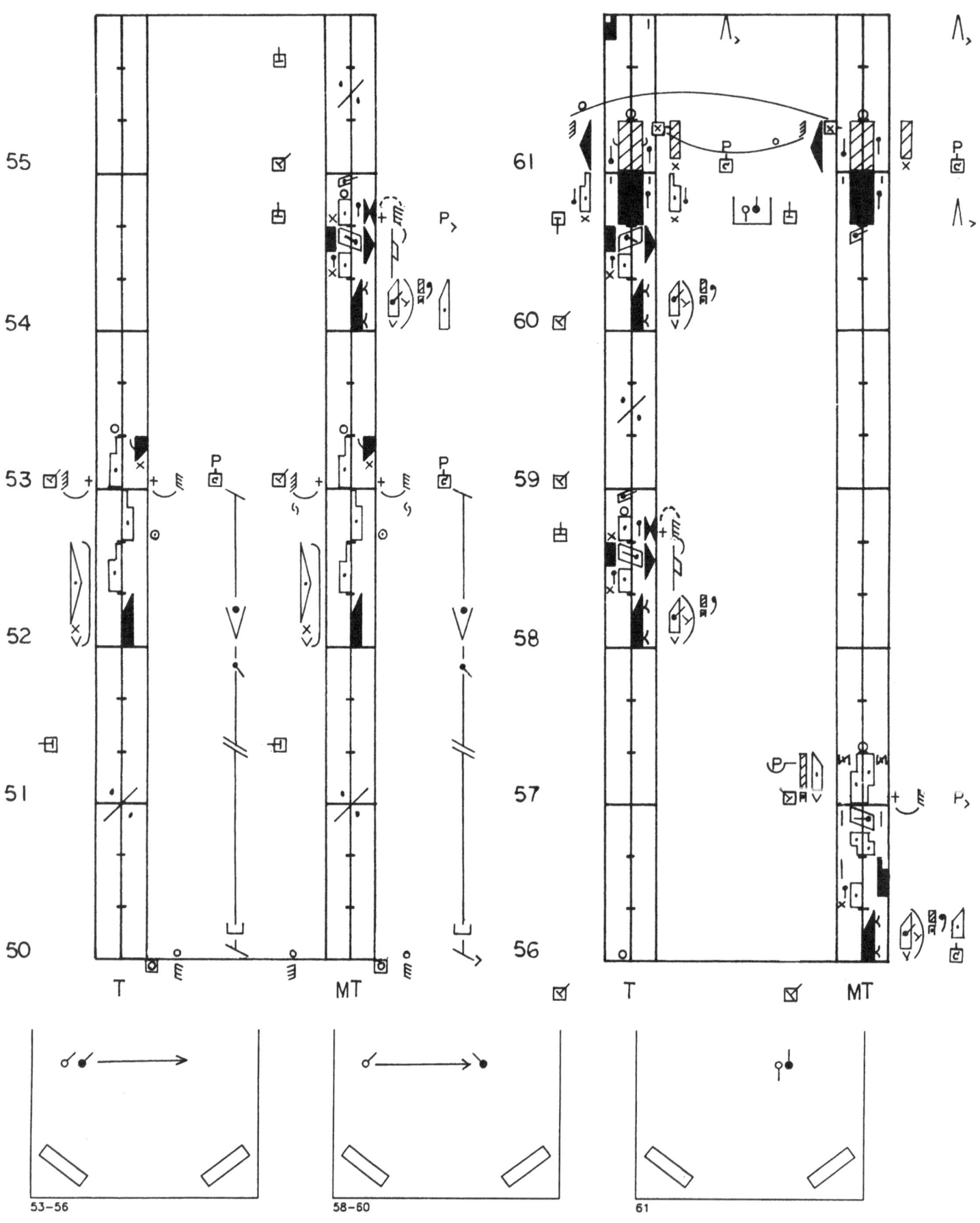

SOIREE MUSICALE

TIROLESE

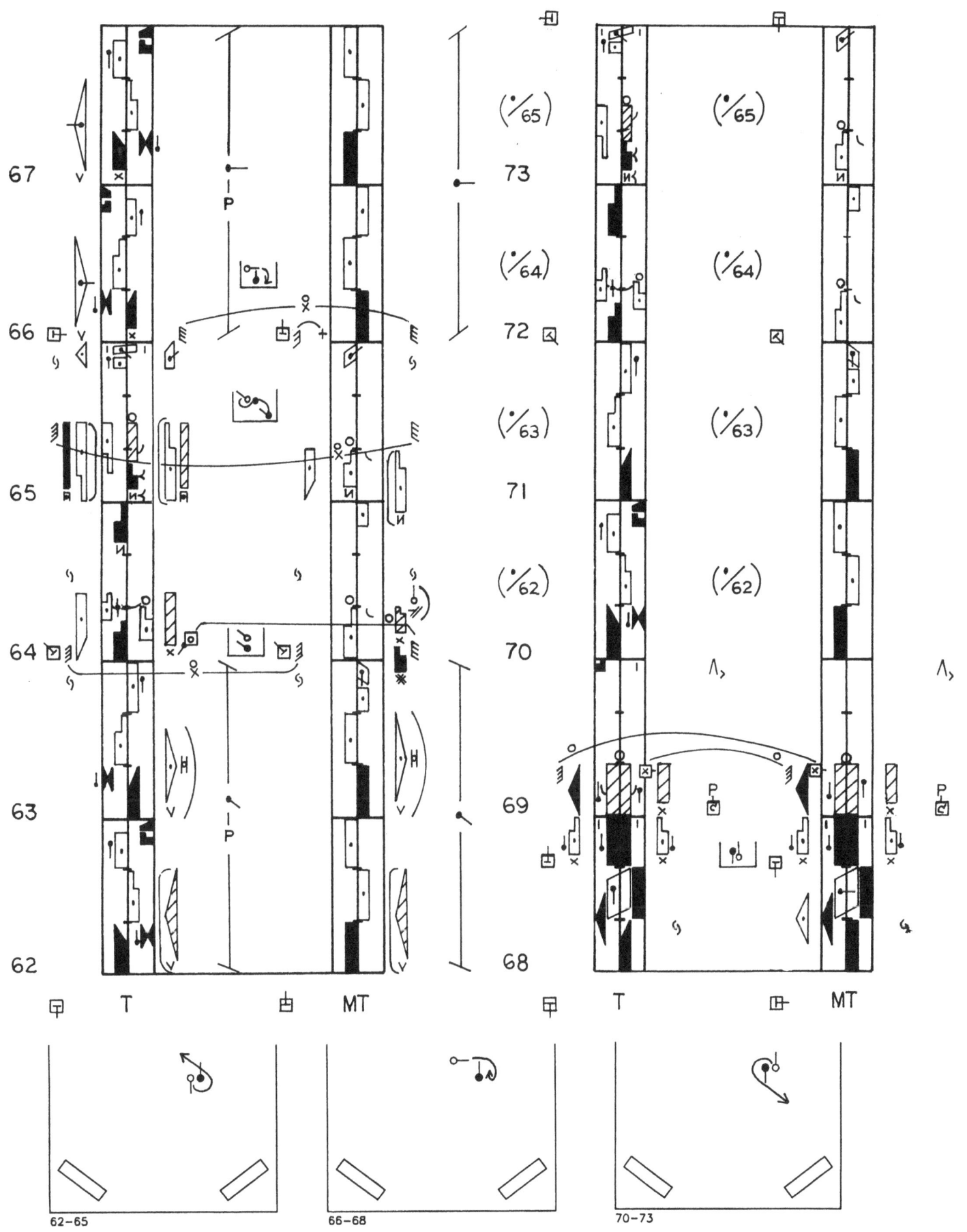

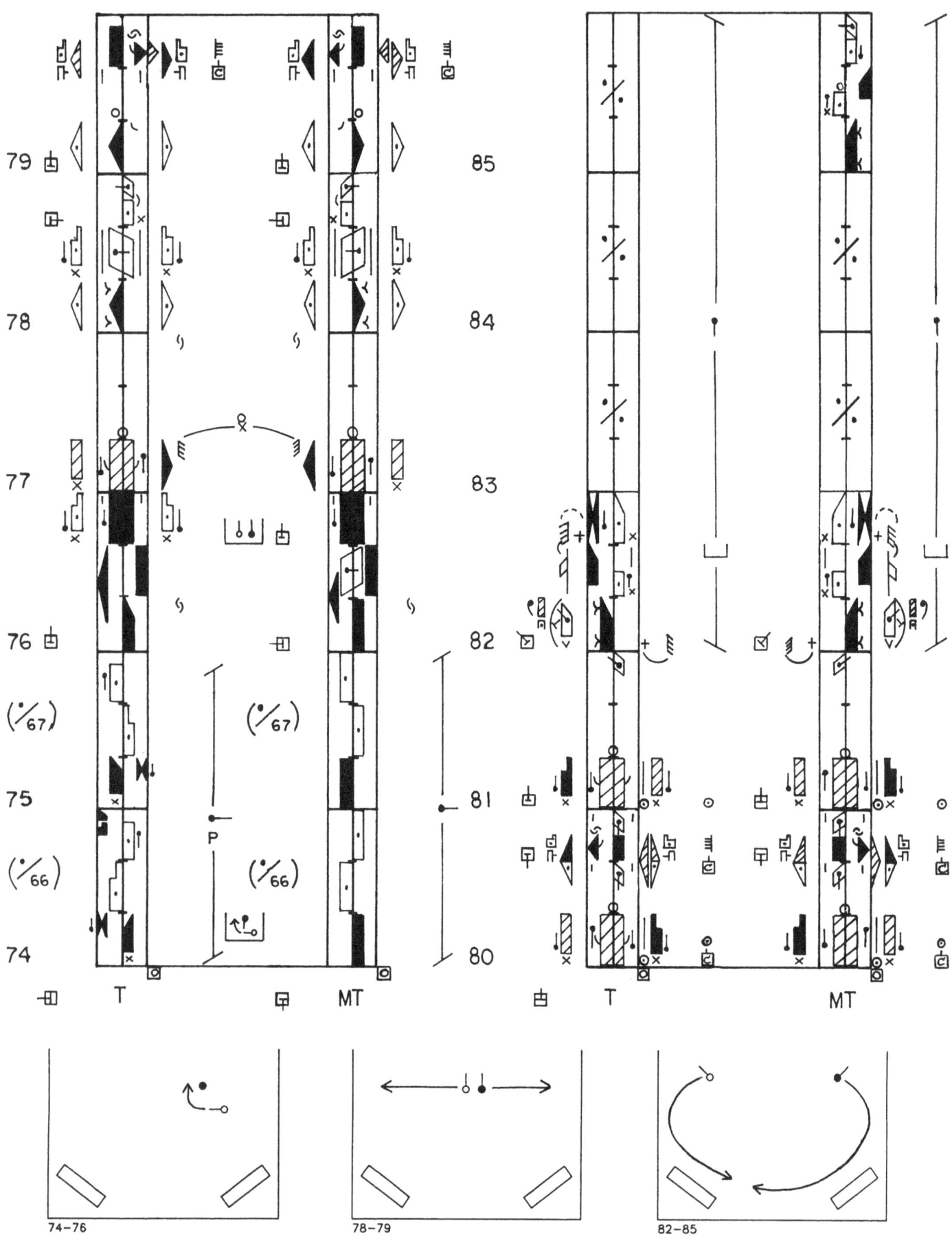

TIROLESE

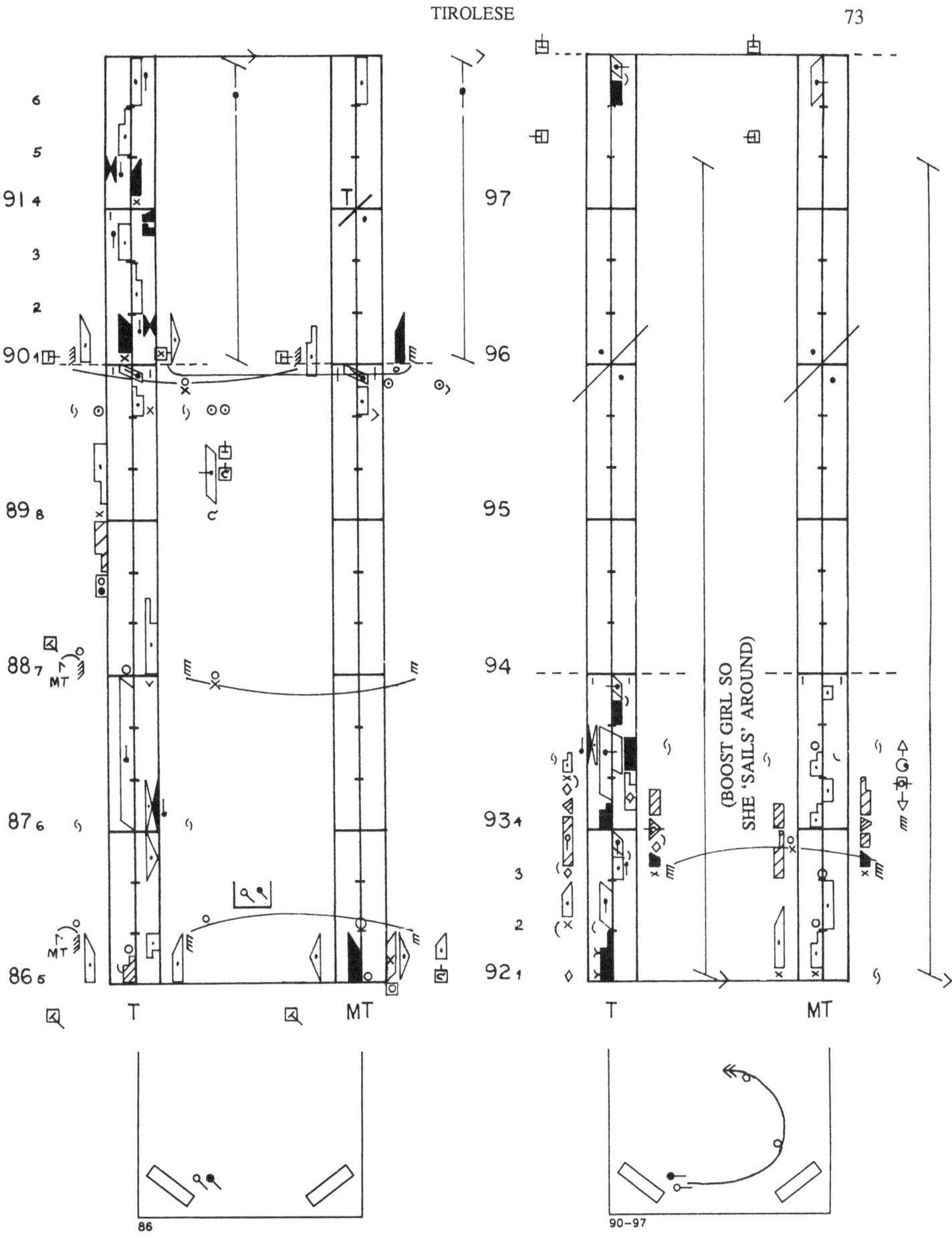

SOIREE MUSICALE

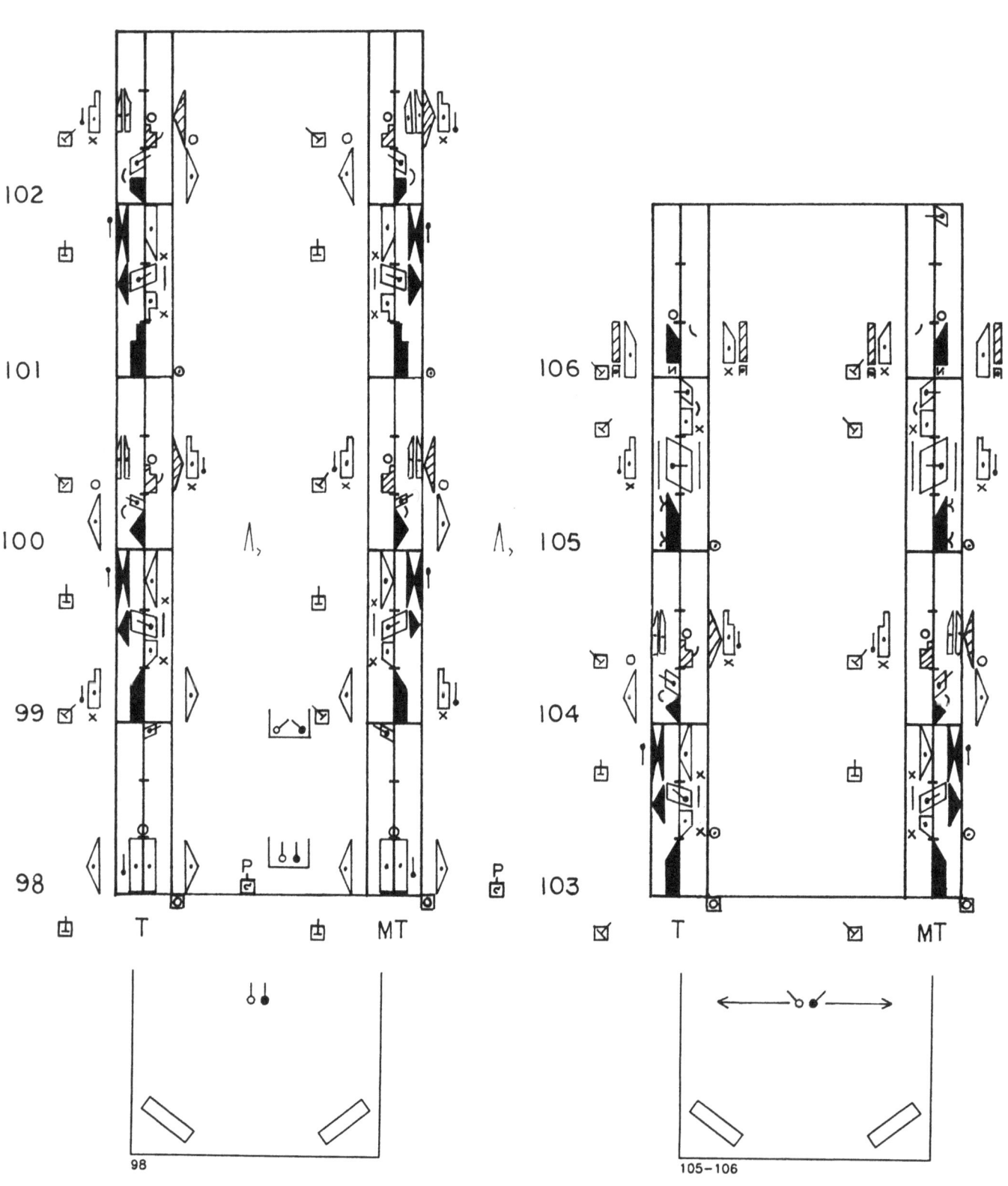

TIROLESE

75

END OF TIROLESE

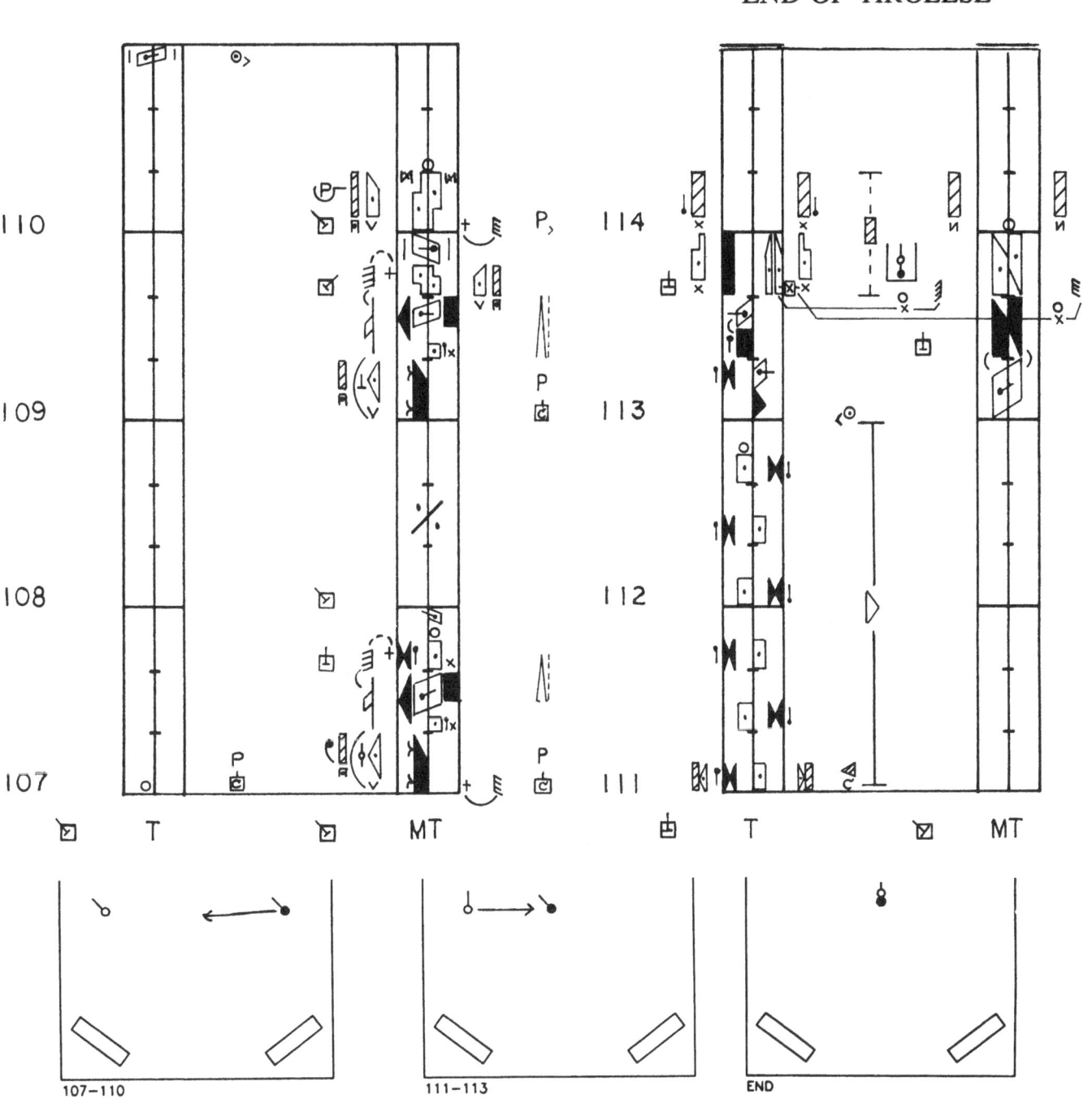

TRANSITION TO BOLERO

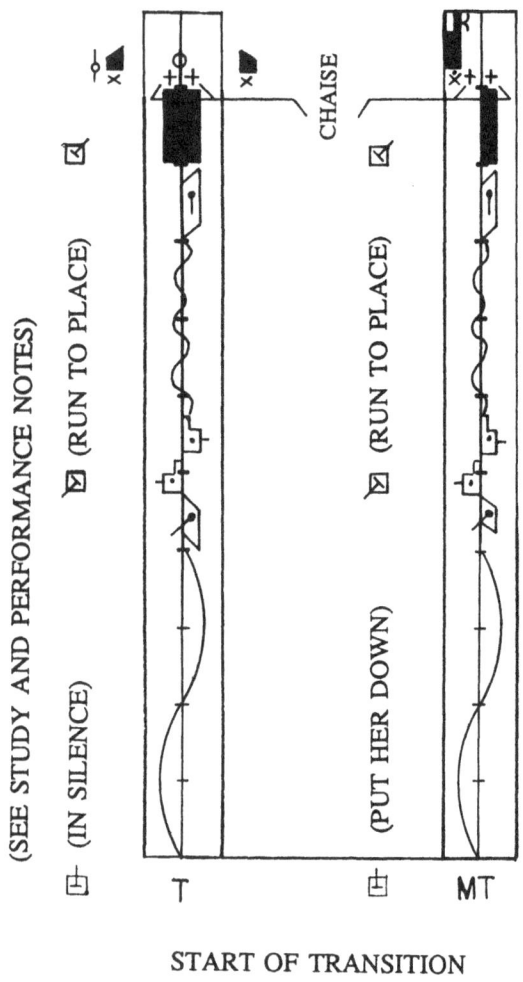

START OF TRANSITION

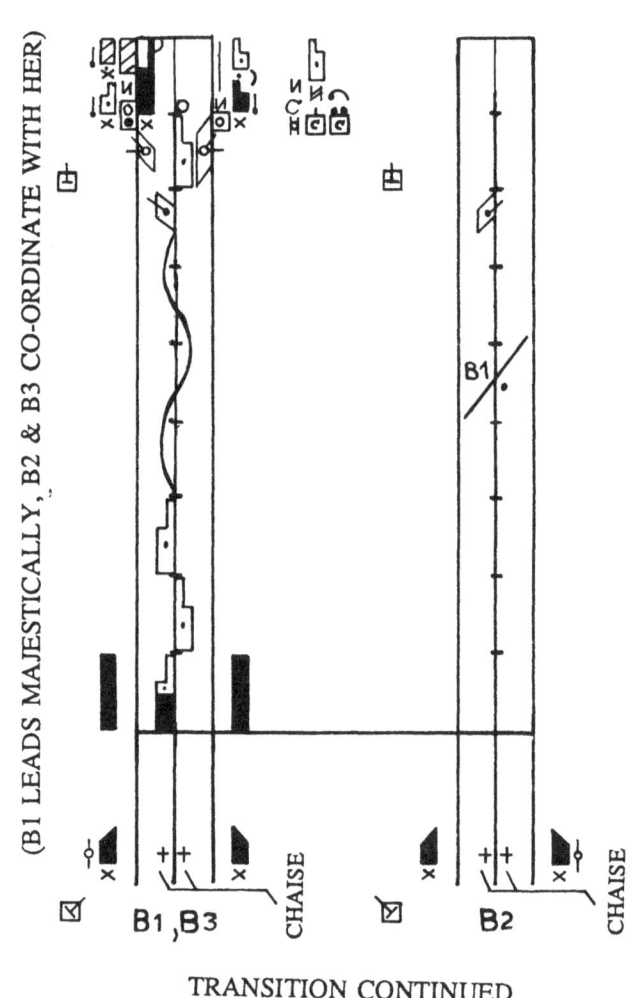

TRANSITION CONTINUED

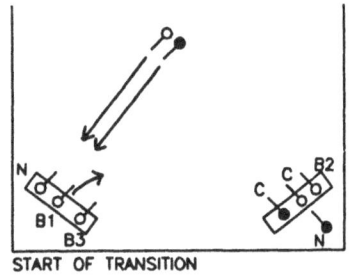

START OF TRANSITION

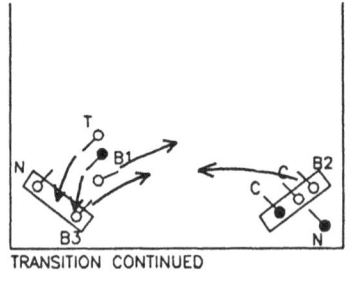

TRANSITION CONTINUED

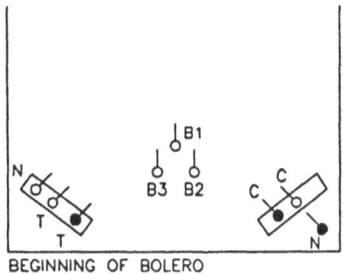

BEGINNING OF BOLERO

Meas. 1
The Scottish Theatre Ballet.
The Bolero ladies mesmerize the audience.
Dancers (L to R): Amanda Olivier, Anne Allan, Sally Collard-Gentle in the foreground;
Michael Beare (seated), Anthony Parnell (standing);
Patricia Rianne, Hilary Debden (seated), Harold King (standing).

Meas. 1, ct. 3
The Joffrey Ballet Company.
The 'teasing step'.
Women (L to R): Rochelle Zide, Brunhilda Ruiz, Suzanne Hammons.
Richard Beaty seated.

(Anthony Crickmay)

Meas. 22, ct. 1
(and Meas. 44, ct.1)
The Scottish Theatre Ballet.
Before the sudden swivel, an imperious pose.
Dancers (L to R): Amanda Olivier, Anne Allan, Sally Collard-Gentle.

Meas. 35, ct. 2
The Joffrey Ballet Company.
Rochelle Zide as B1 in a moment from her solo as she circles the stage.

(Will Rapport)

(Anthony Crickmay)

Meas. 48
The Scottish Theatre Ballet.
The concluding pose.
Dancers (L to R): Amanda Olivier, Anne Allan (kneeling), Sally Collard-Gentle.

BOLERO

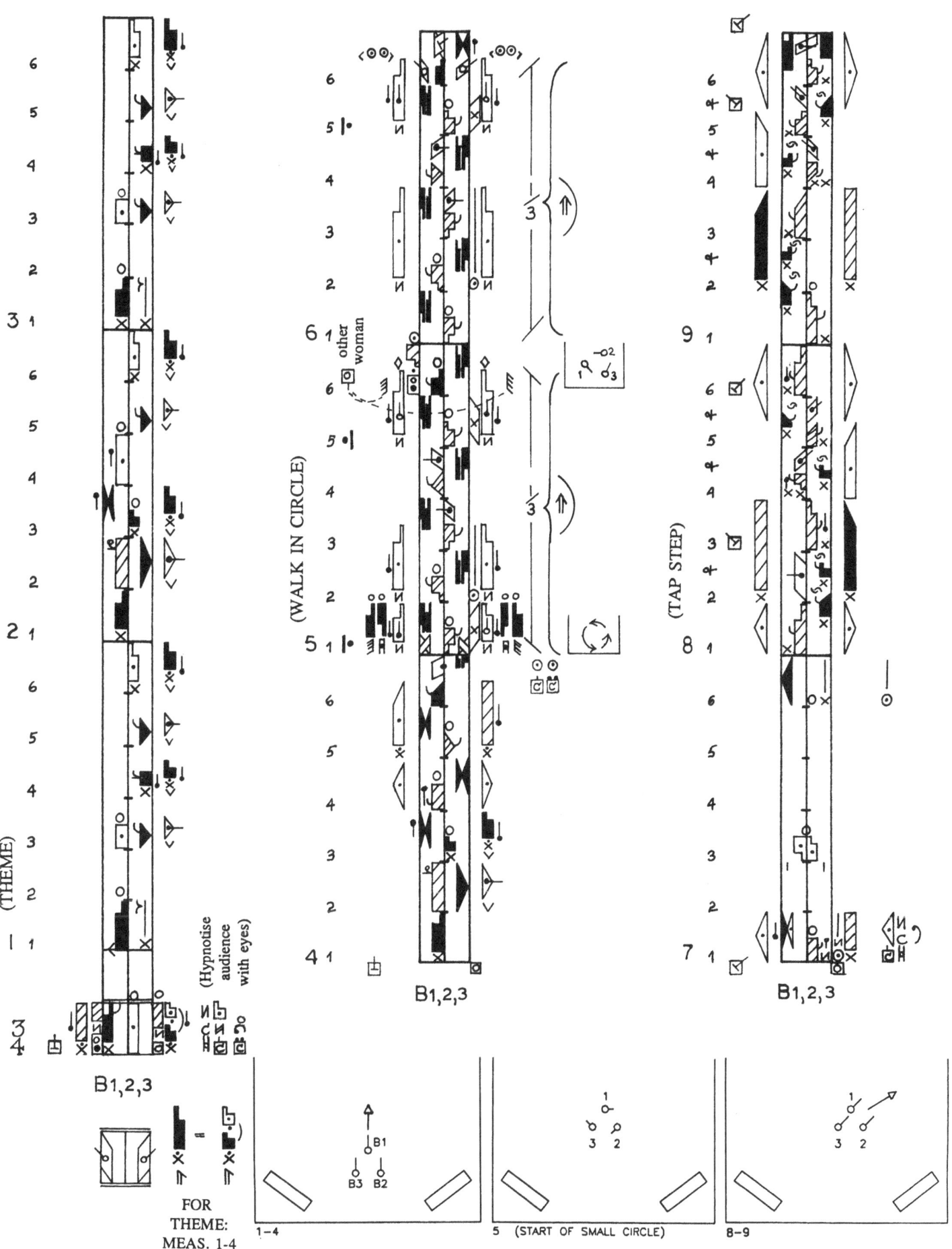

SOIREE MUSICALE

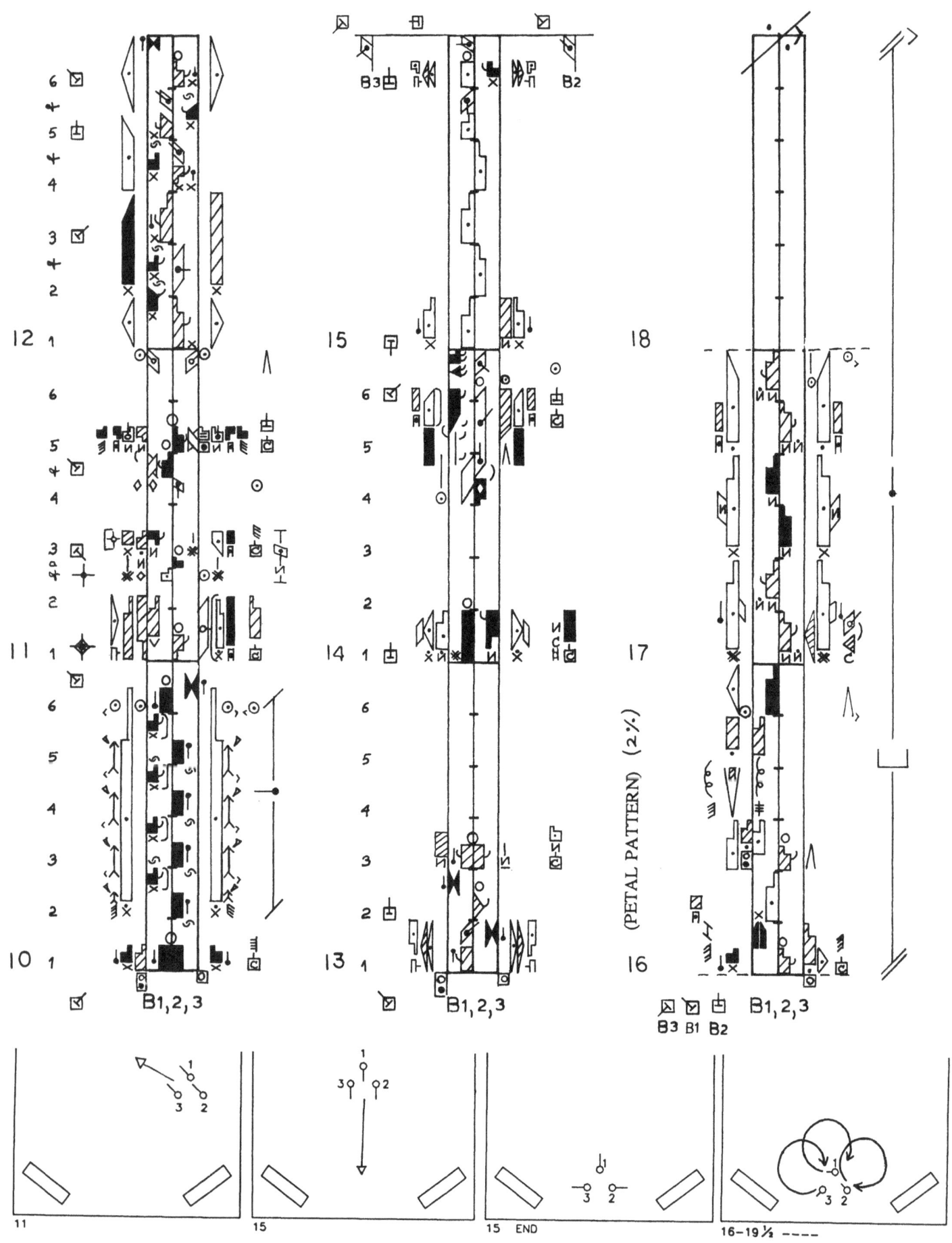

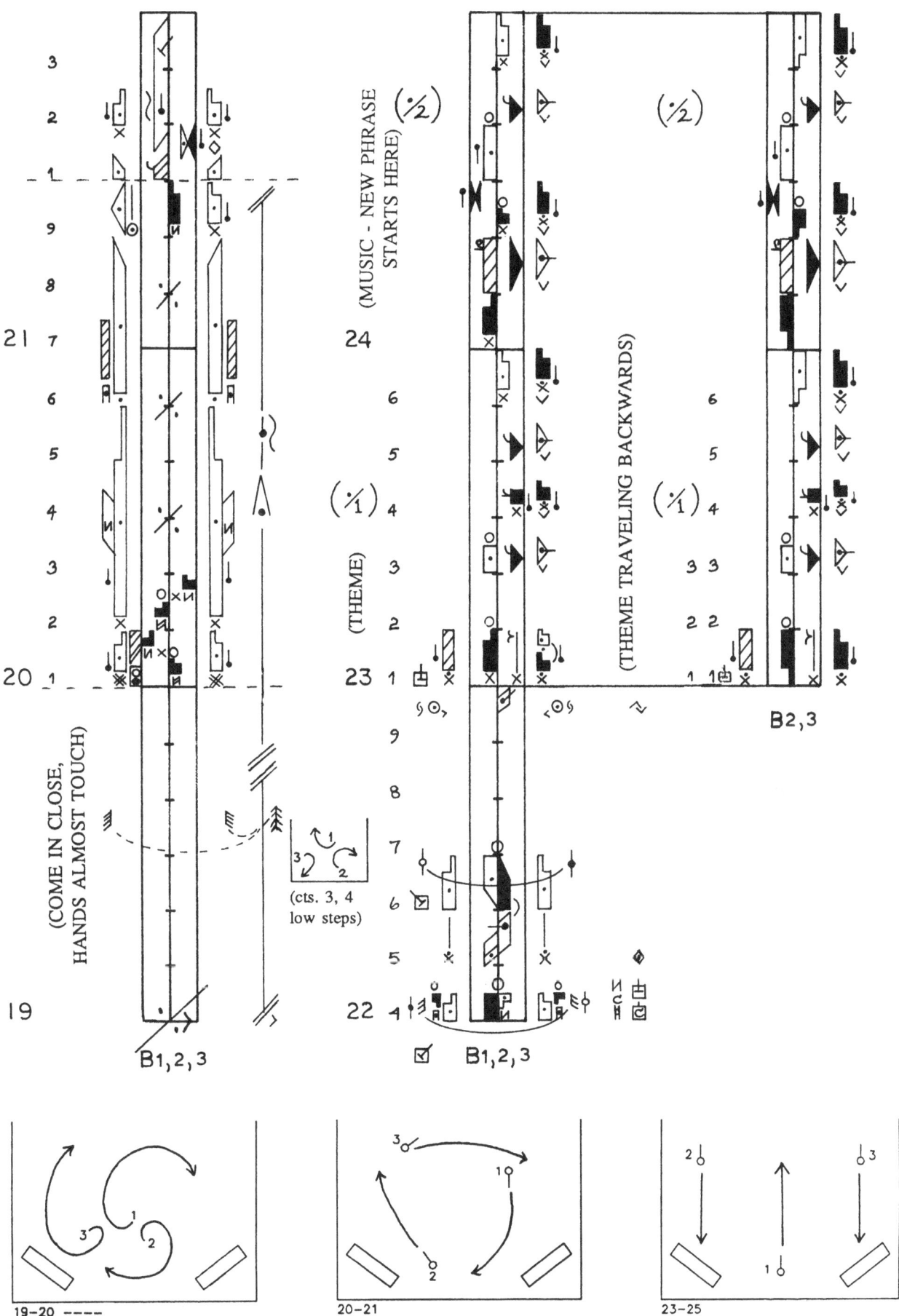

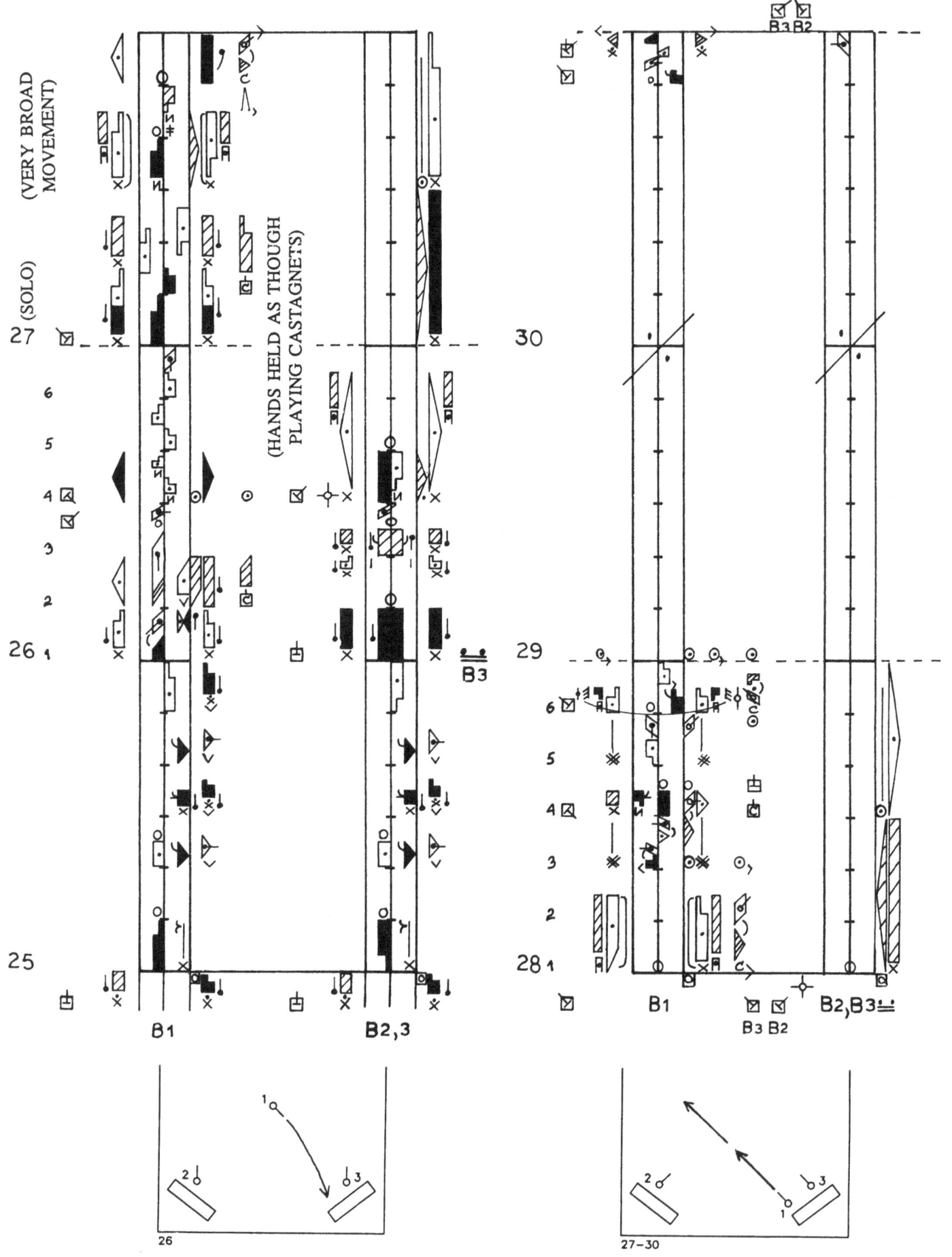

BOLERO

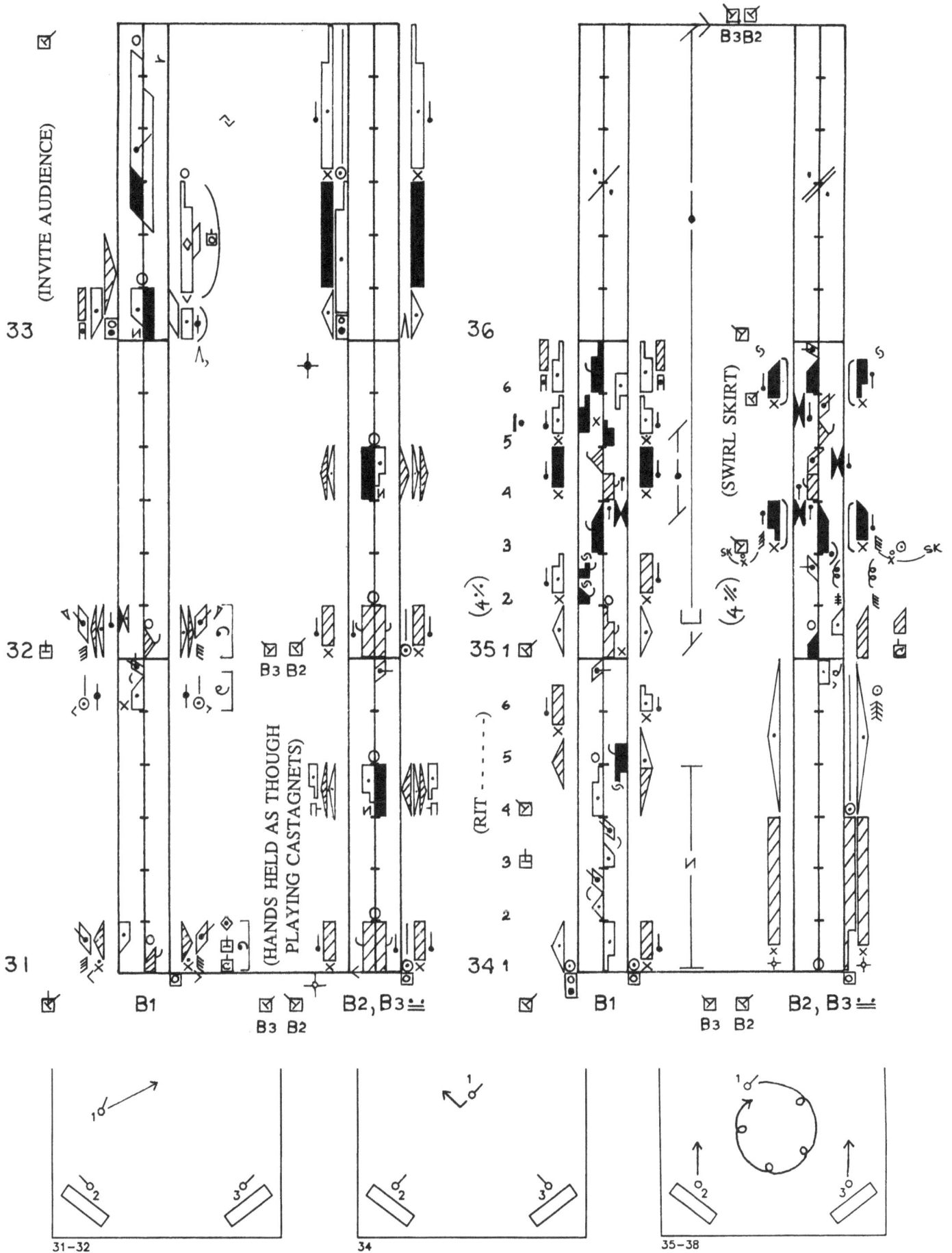

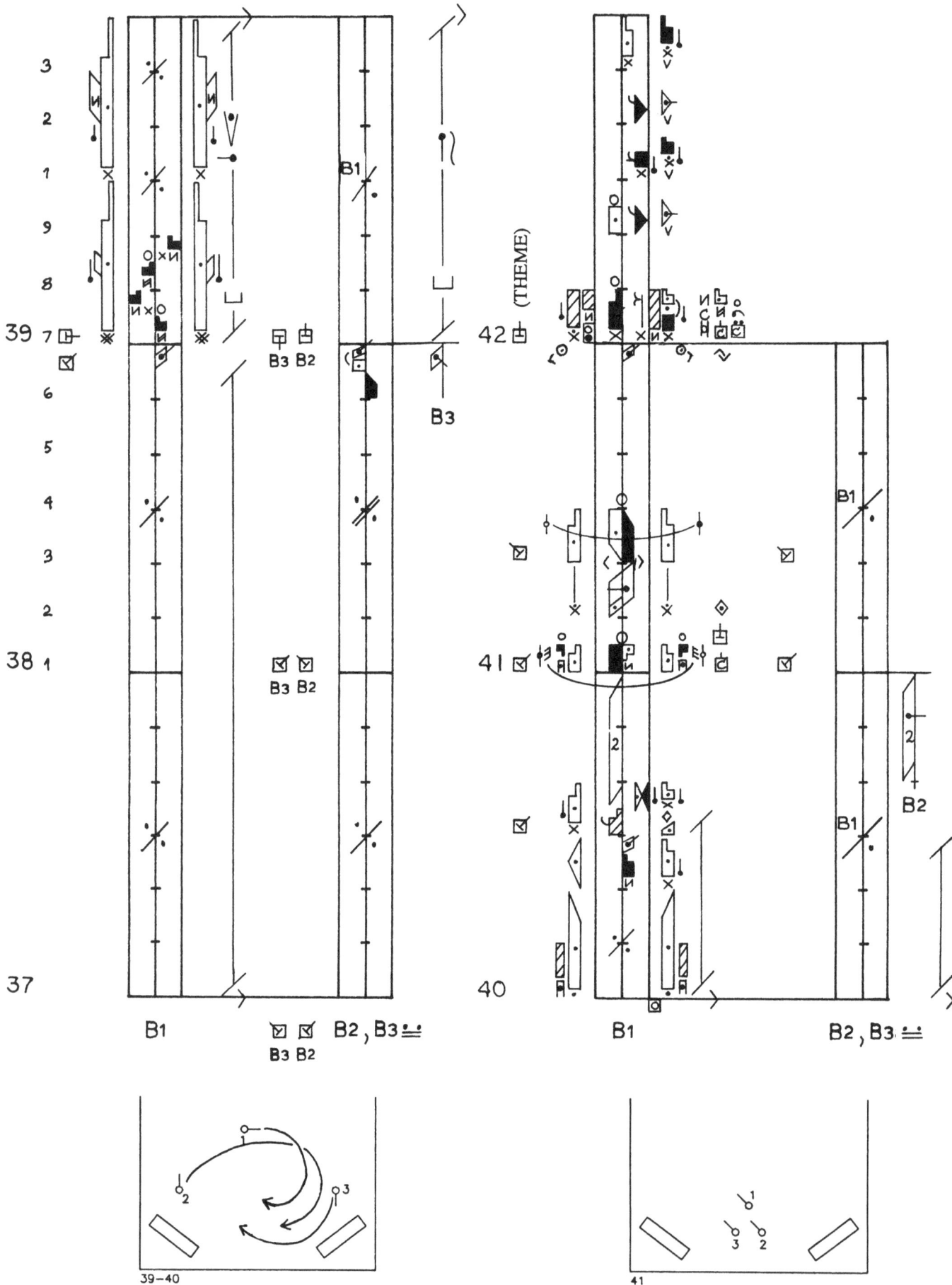

BOLERO END OF BOLERO

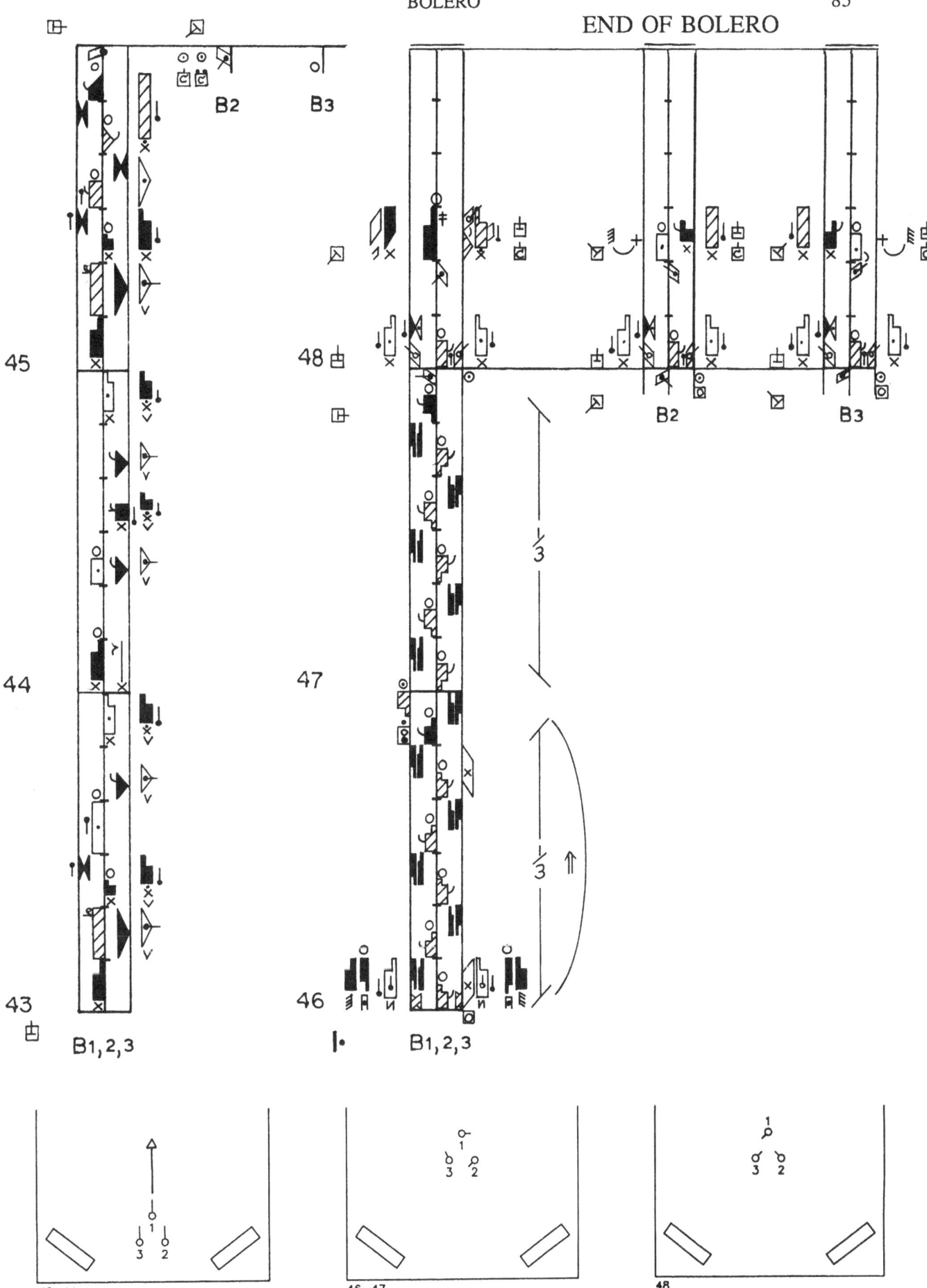

TRANSITION TO NEAPOLITAN

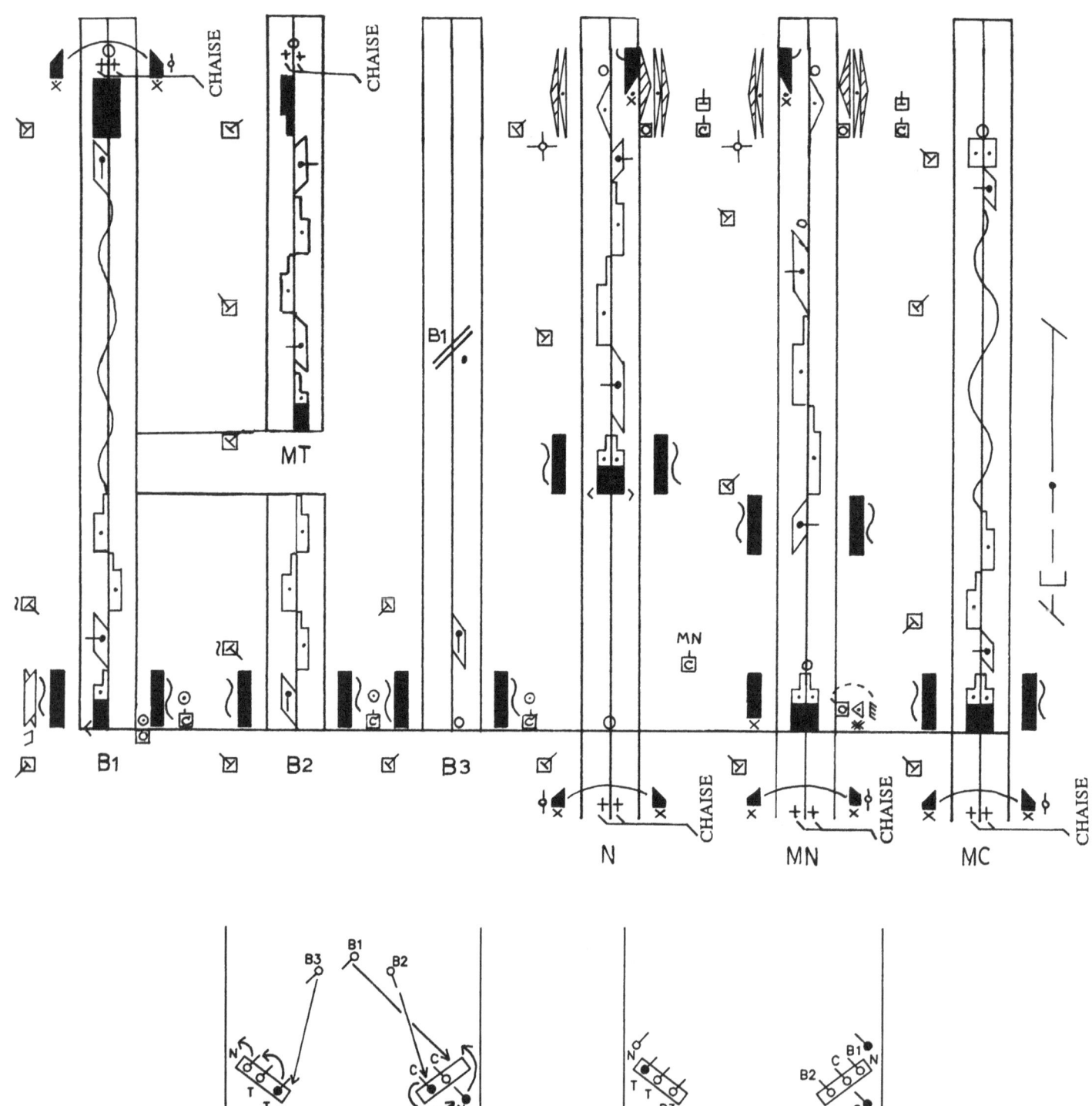

NEAPOLITAN

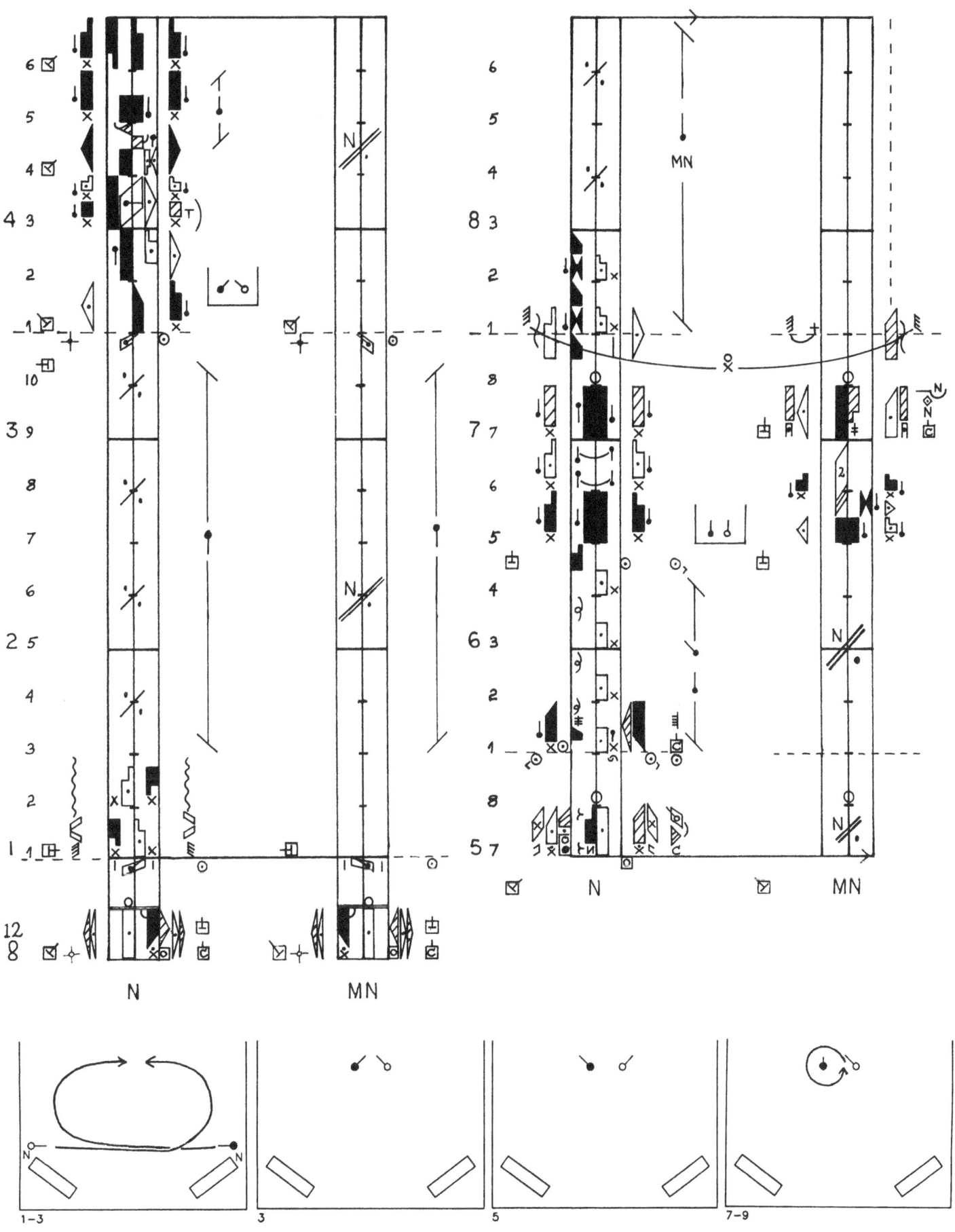

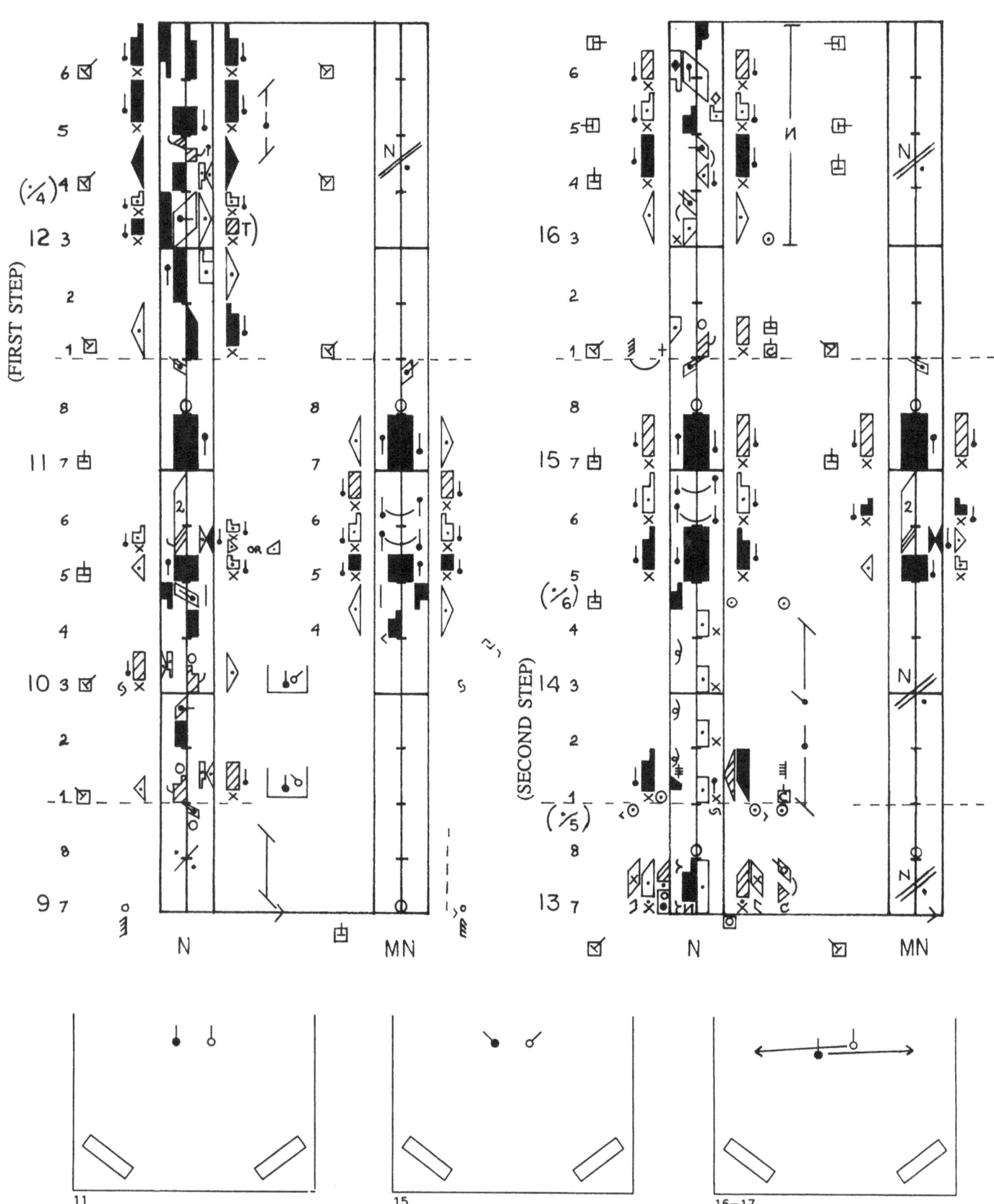

NEAPOLITAN

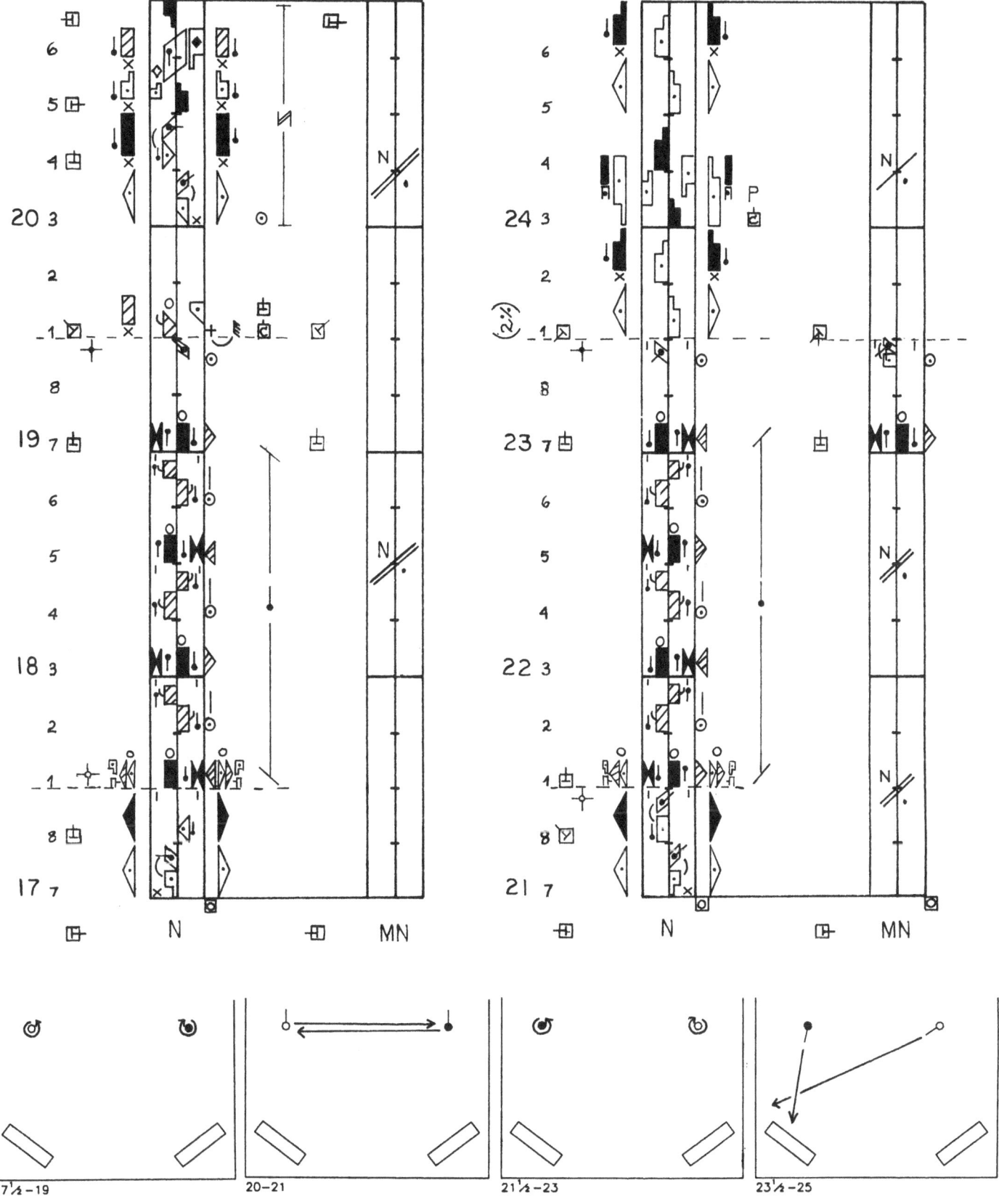

Meas. 27, ct. 3
The Scottish Theatre Ballet.
The man's 'stag' jump as they progress across the diagonal.
Michael Beare dancing with Hilary Debden.
In the background (L group): Anne Allan and Anthony Parnell (standing),
Amanda Olivier and Elaine McDonald (seated);
(R group): Patricia Rianne and Sally Collard-Gentle (seated), Harold King (standing).

Meas. 40
The Scottish Theatre Ballet.
In this photo the woman takes a more extended *attitude* with more tilt in the torso.
Dancers as above.

(16 count phrase)
25
26
27
28
29
30
31
32
N
MN
N
MN

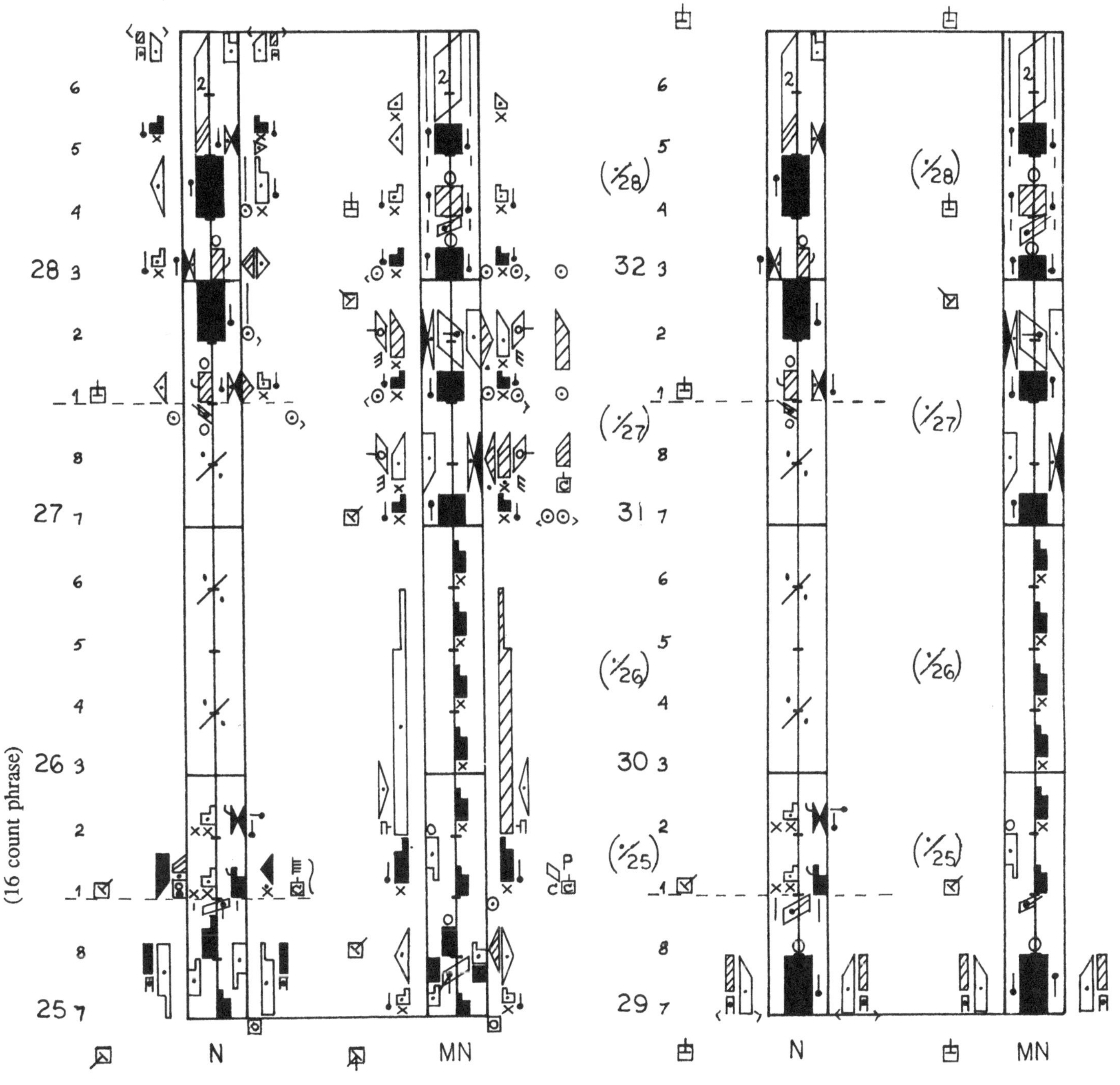

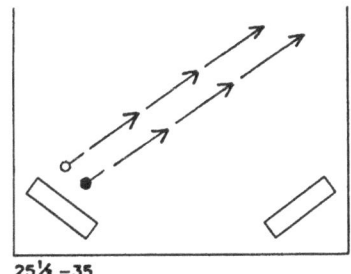

25½ –35

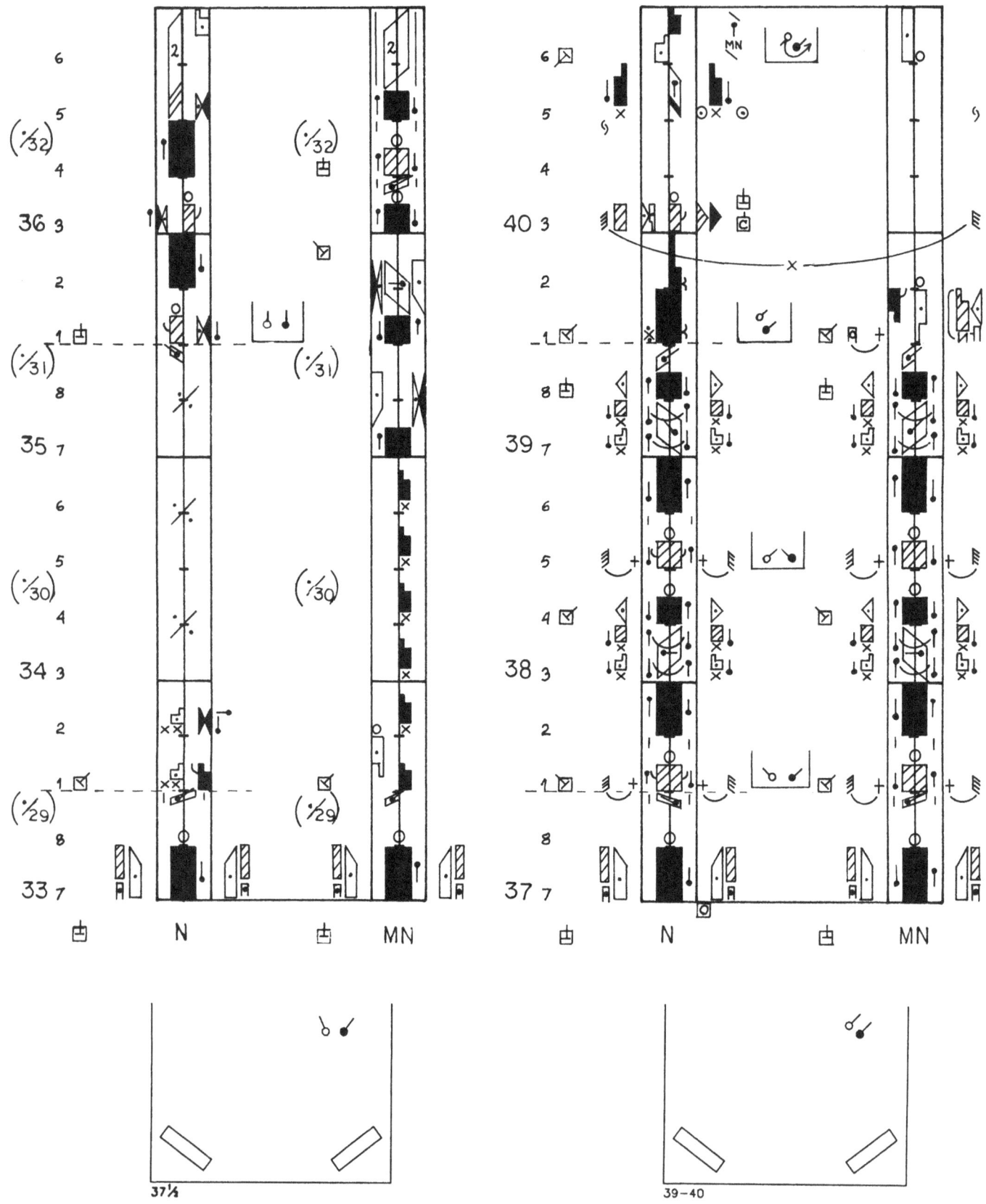

NEAPOLITAN

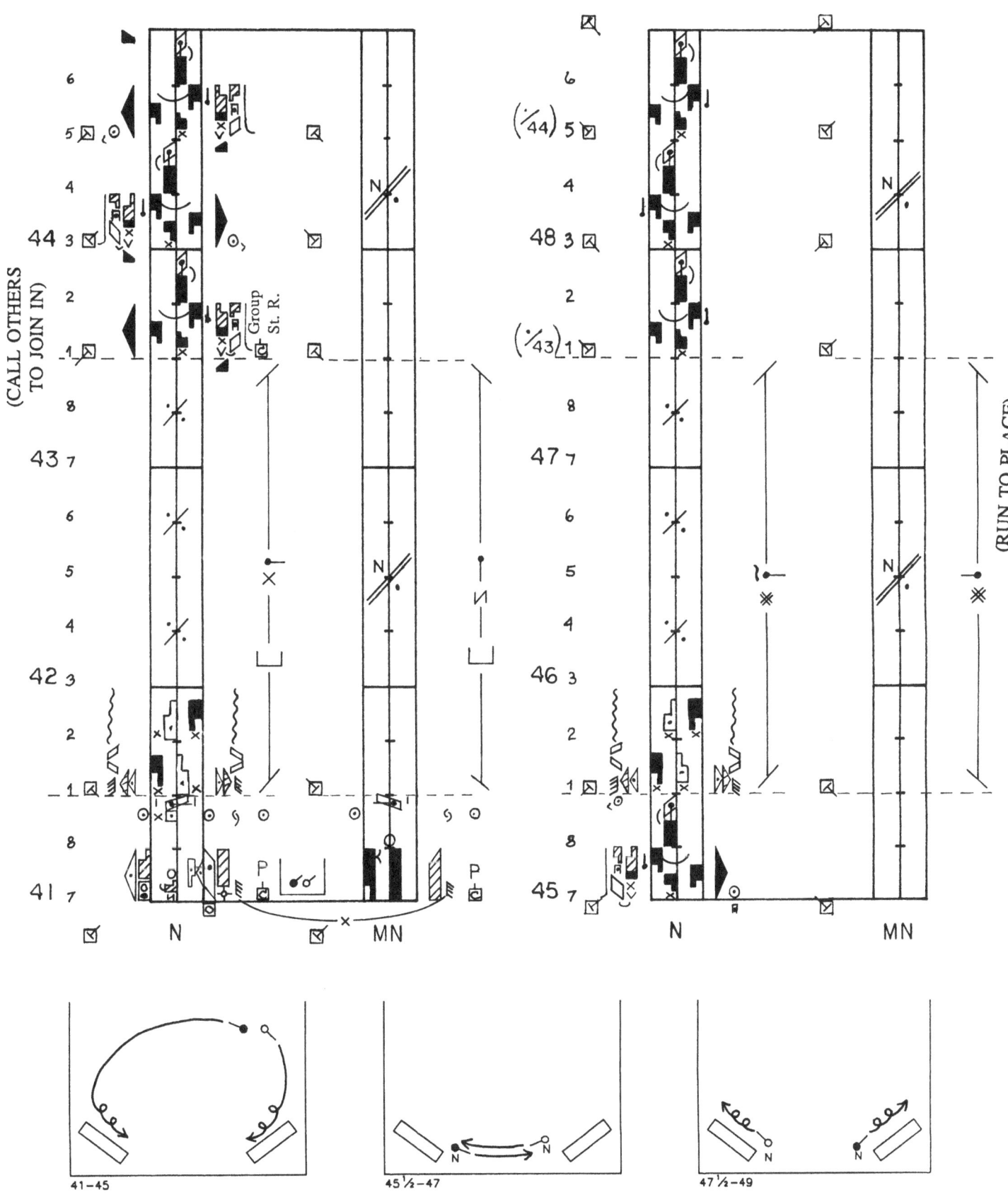

FINALE

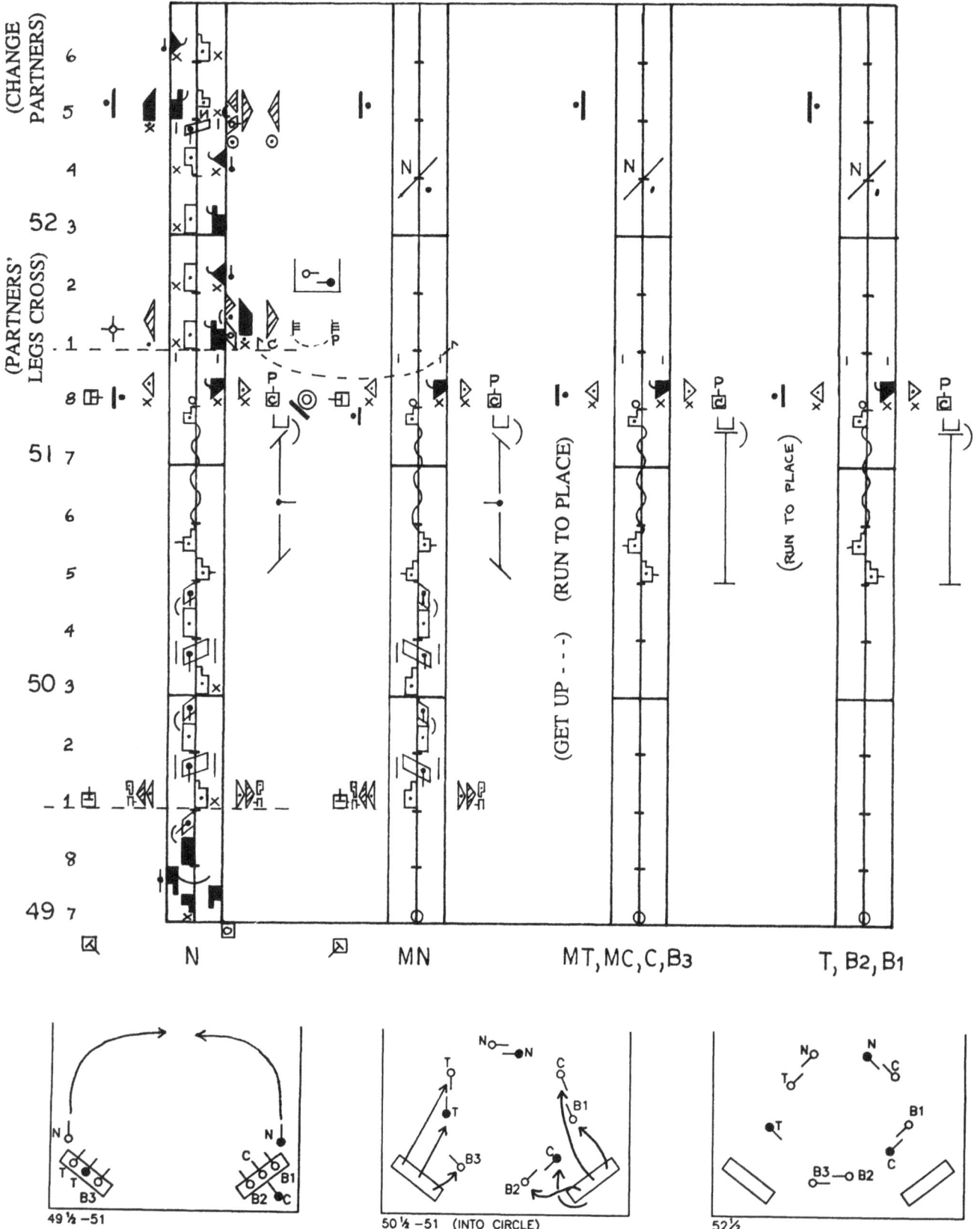

FINALE

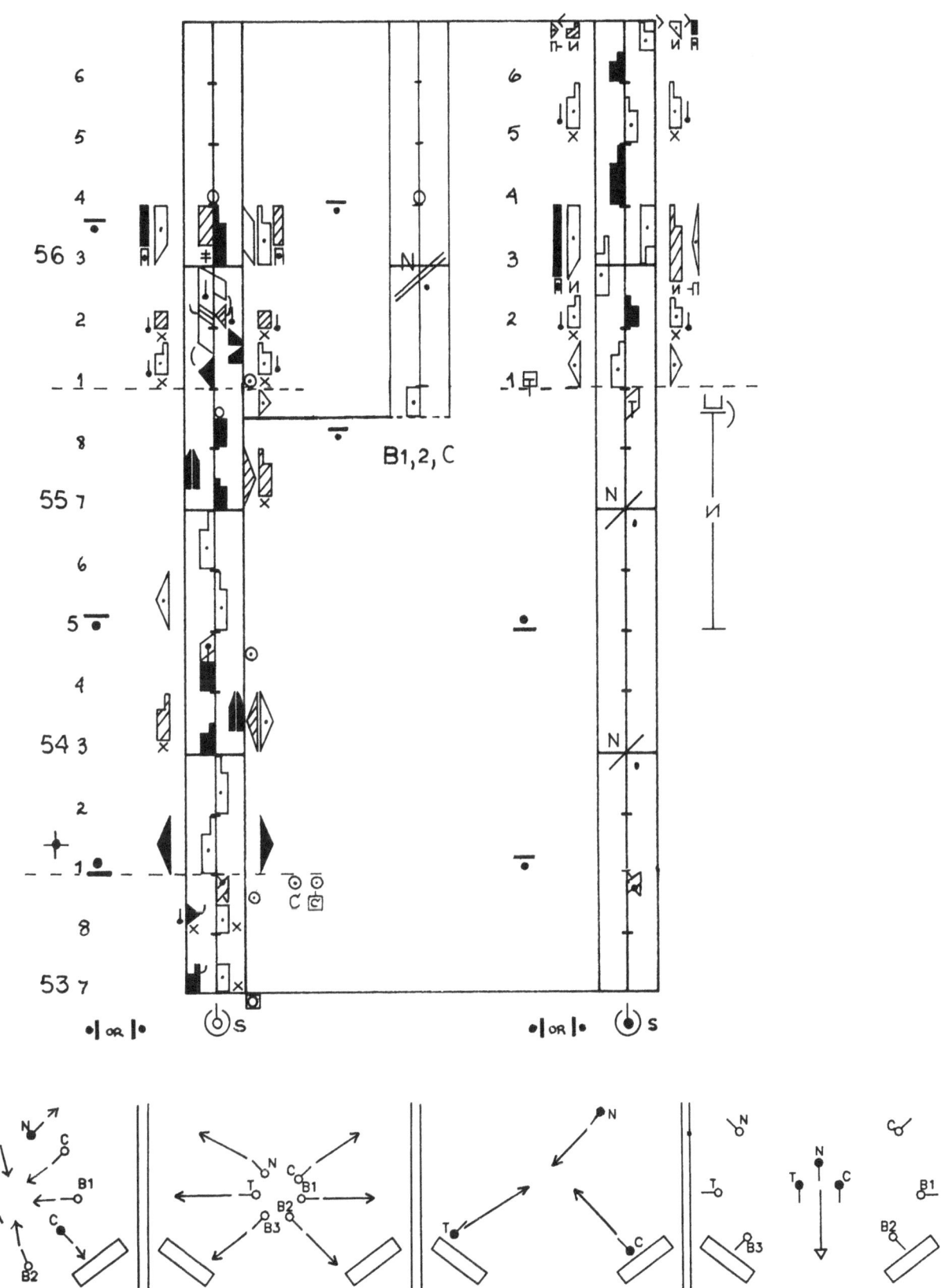

53½ (MEN OUT, WOMEN IN) 54½–55½ (WOMEN OUT) 54½–55½ (MEN IN) 55½–57

96 SOIREE MUSICALE

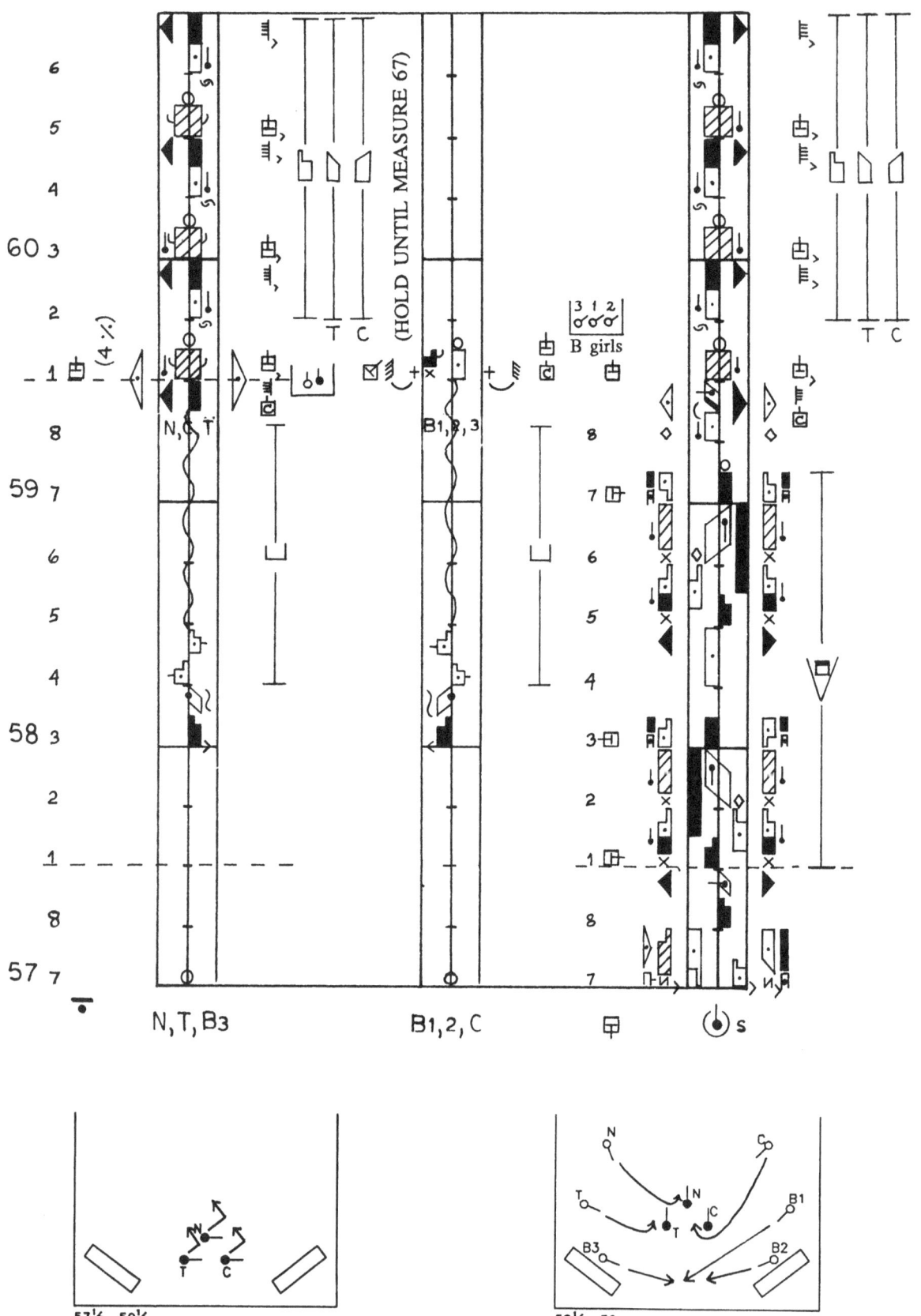

FINALE

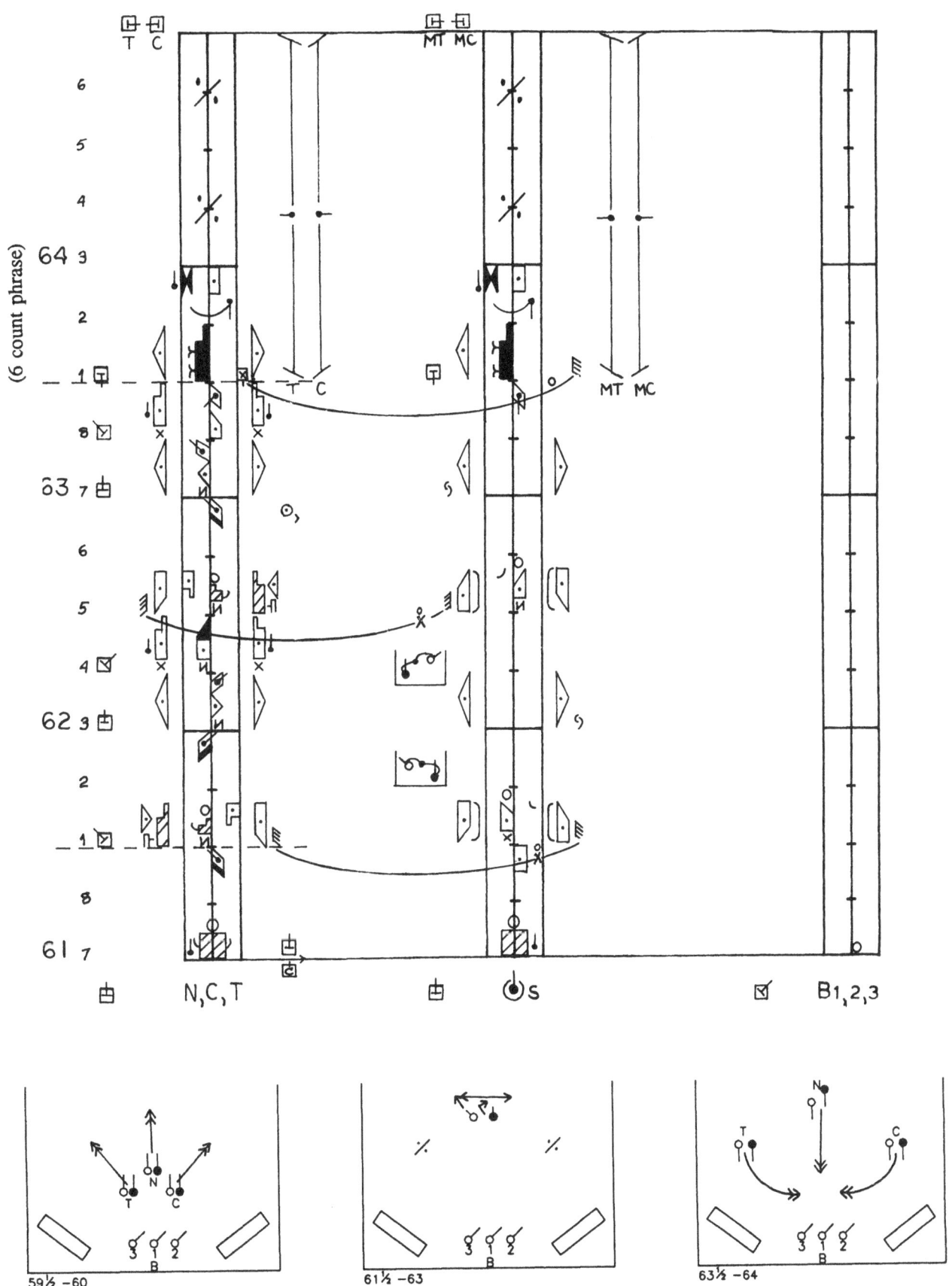

SOIREE MUSICALE

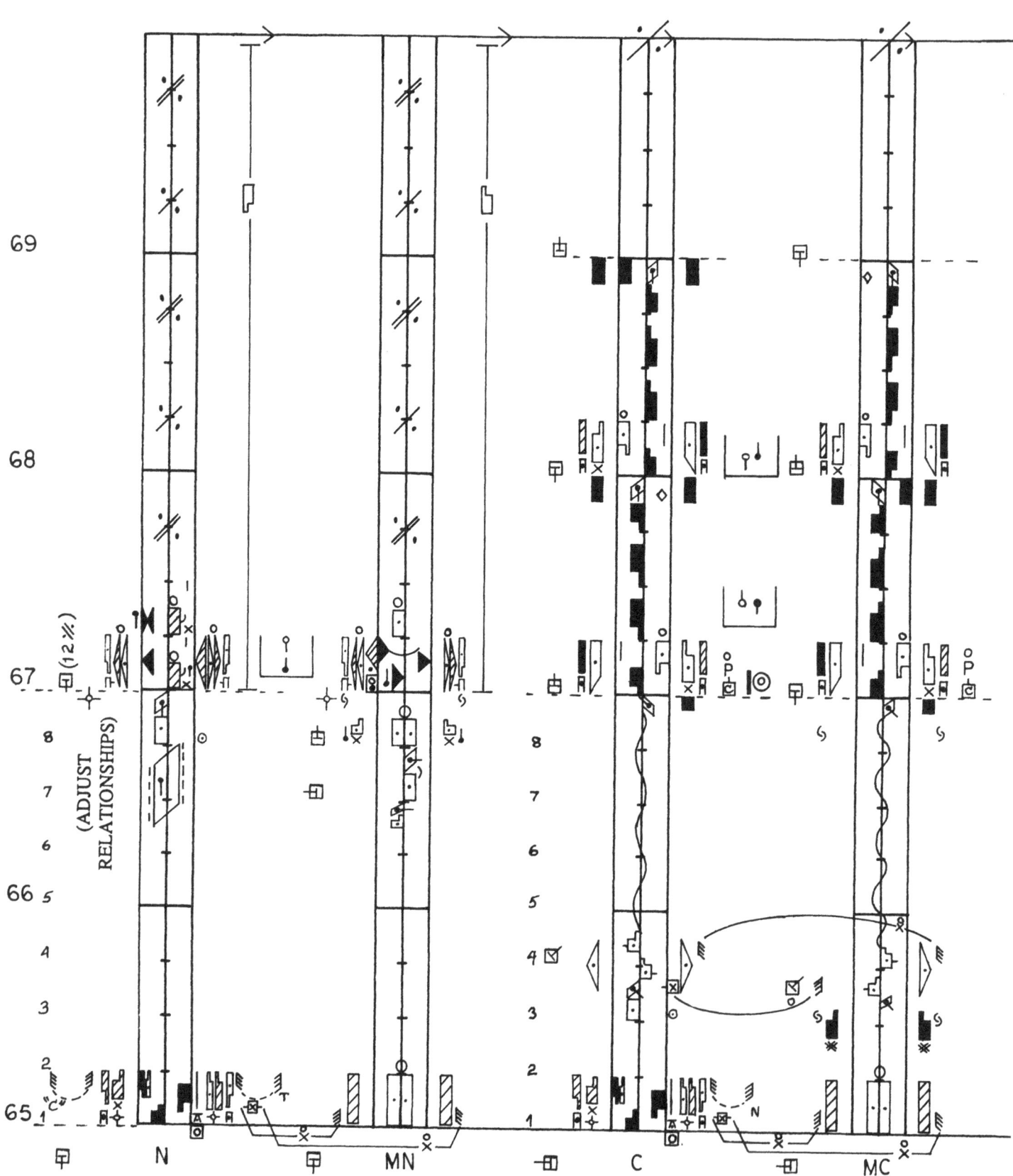

FINALE

99

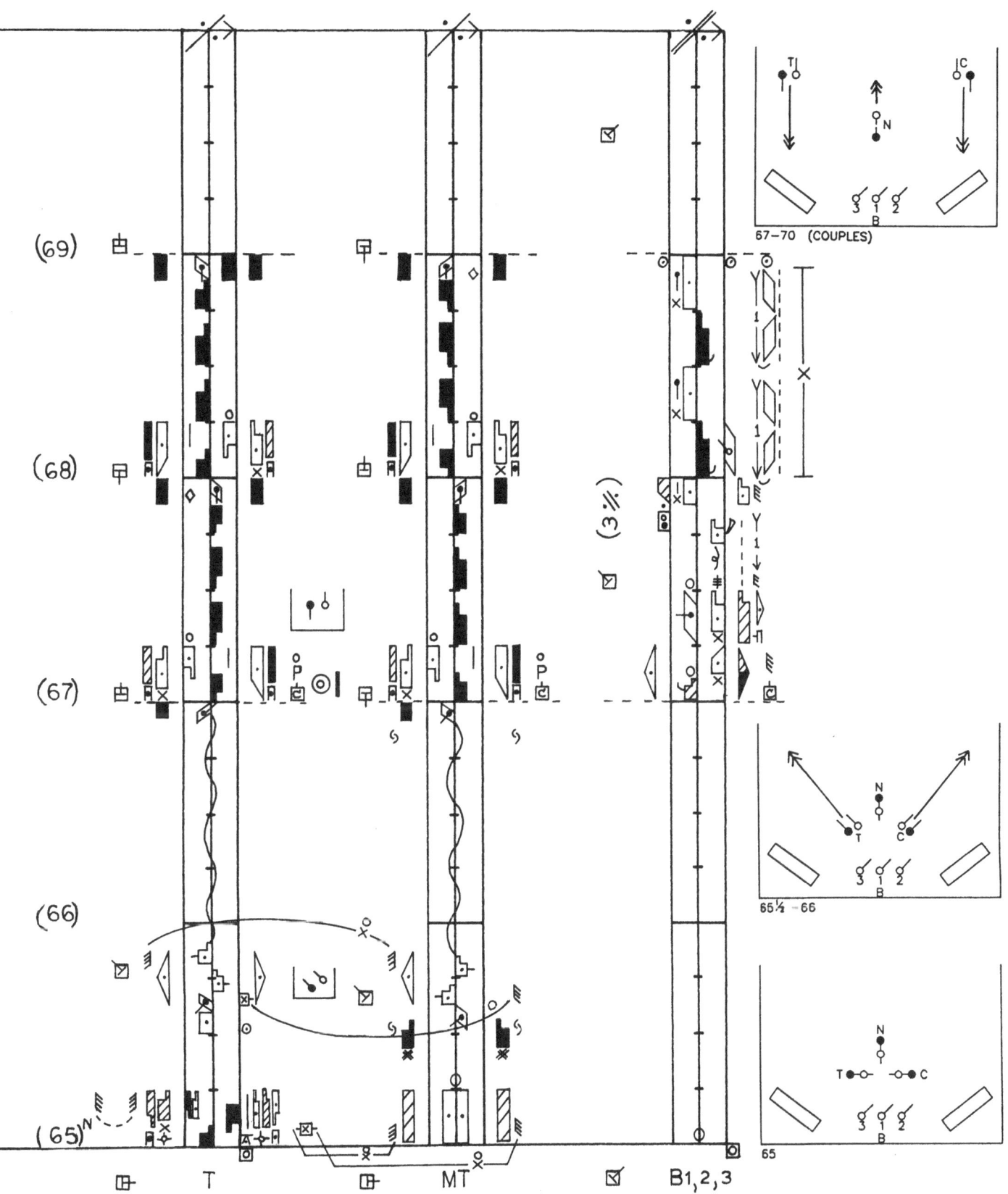

SOIREE MUSICALE

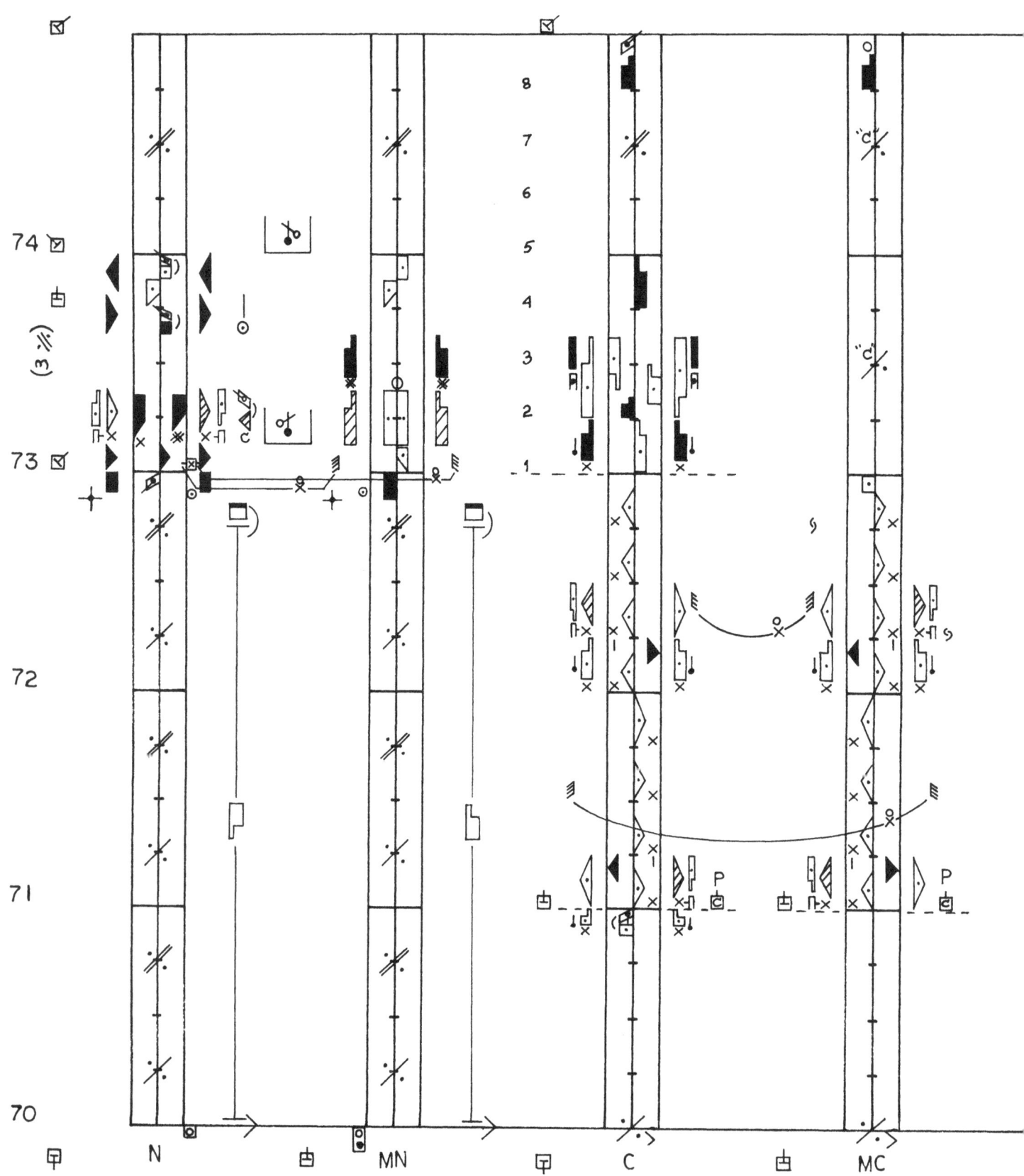

FINALE

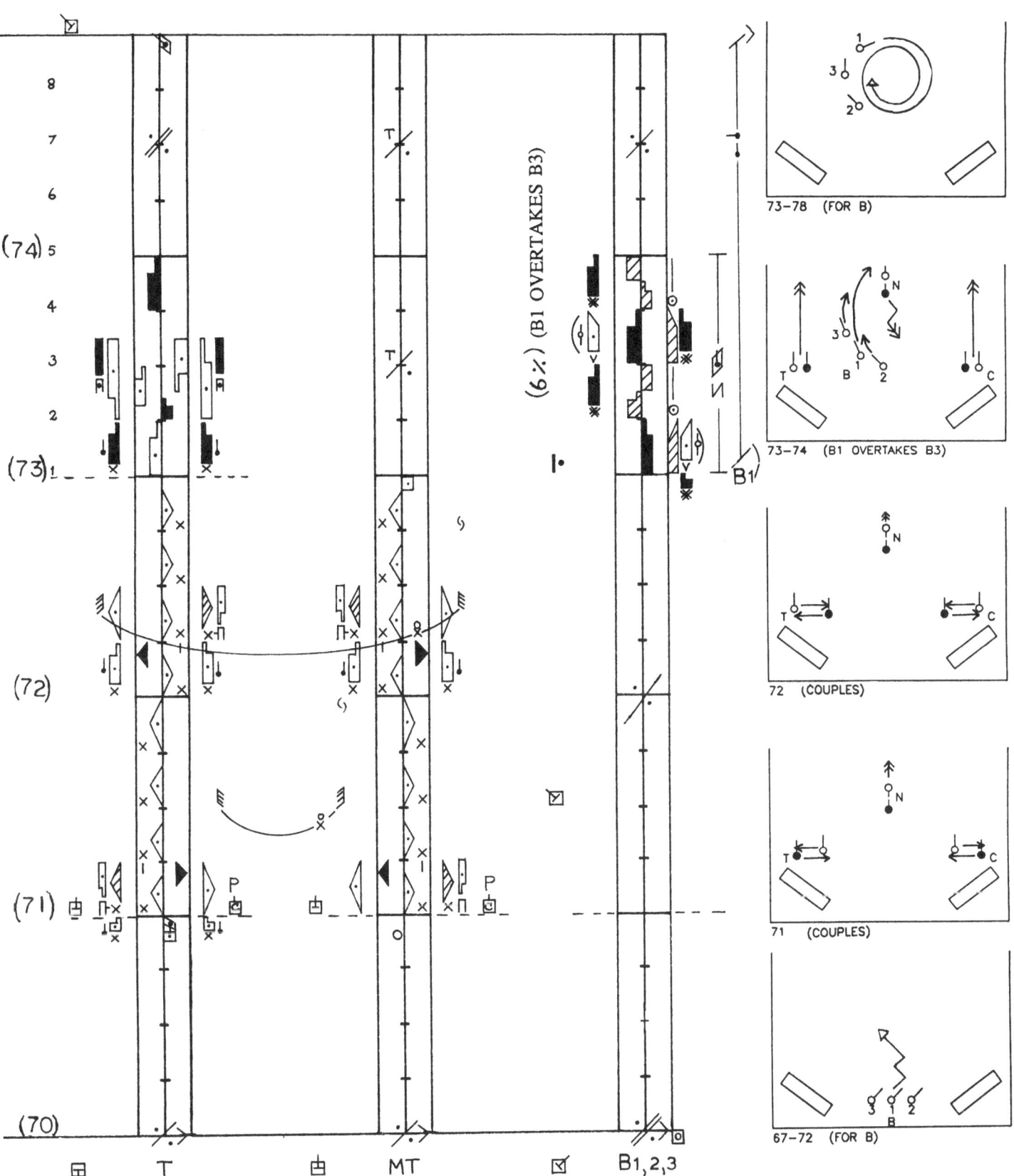

102 *SOIREE MUSICALE*

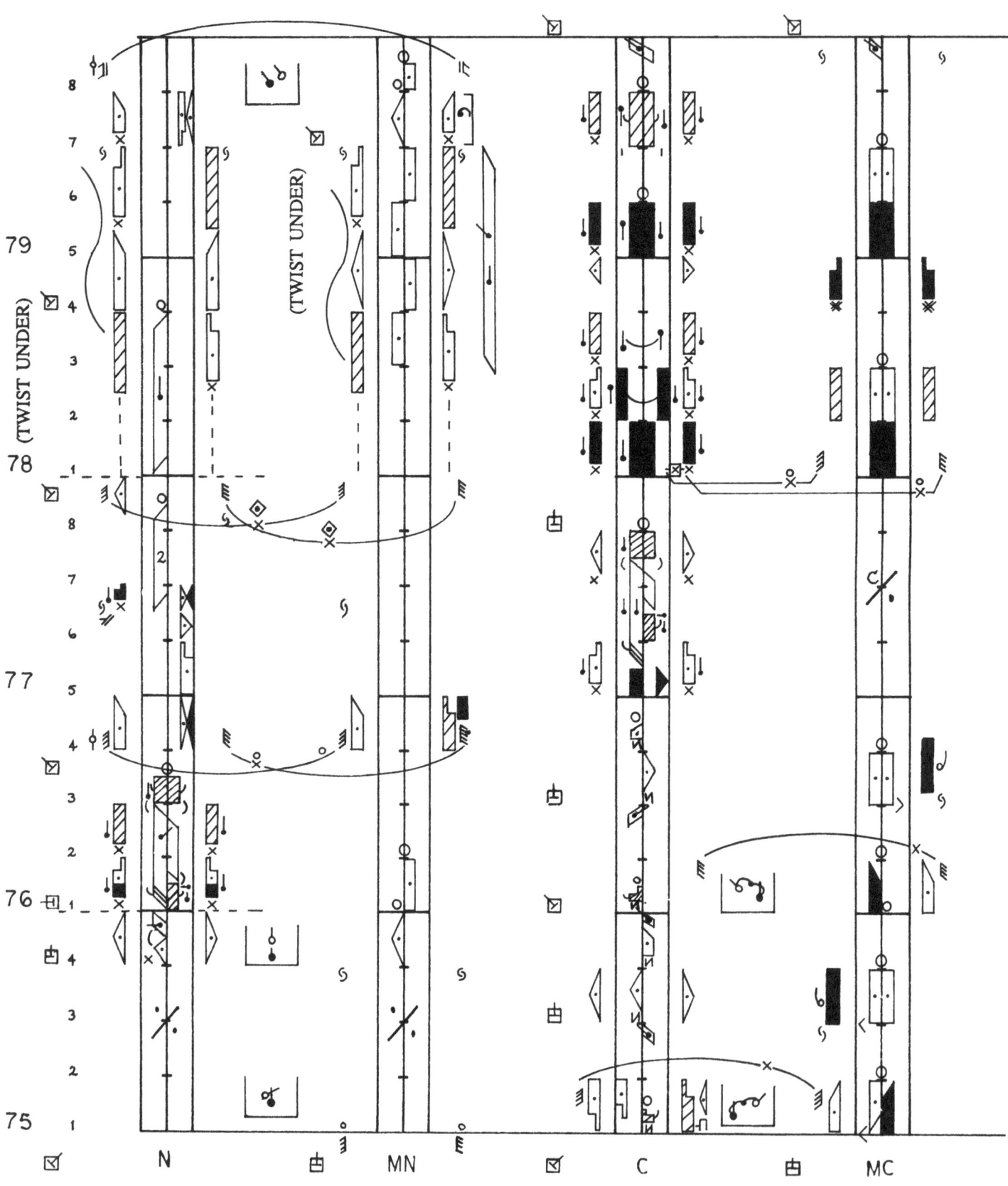

FINALE

103

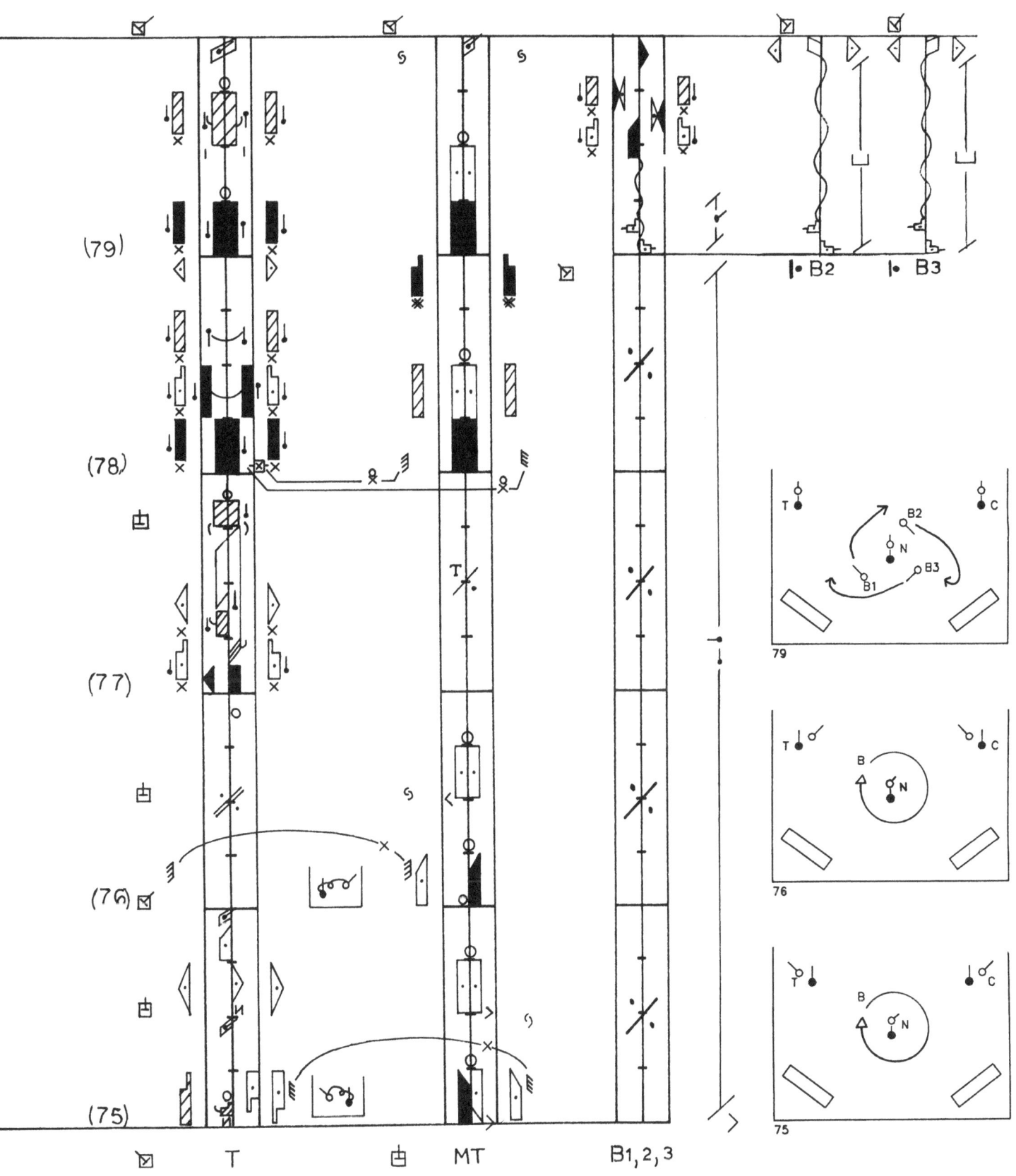

THE END

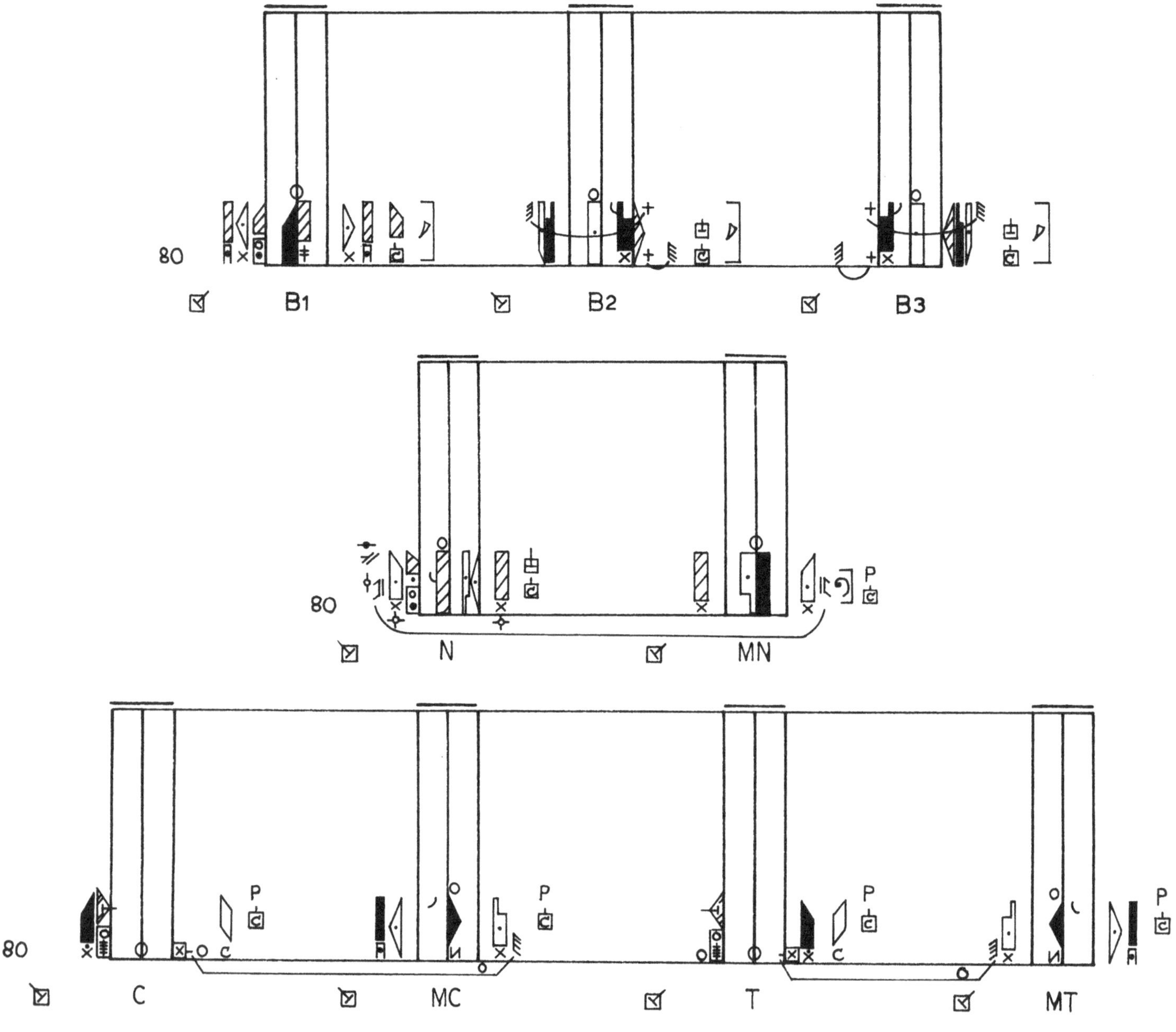

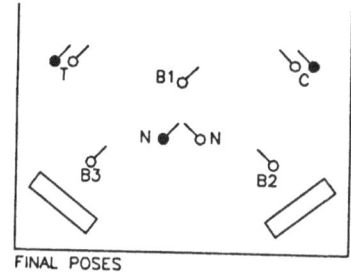

FINAL POSES

FINALE

105

The Final Pose
Ballet Rambert at the Birmingham Repertory Theatre, 1946.
Couples (L to R): Margaret Scott, Stanley Newby - Canzonetta; Michael Bayston, Brenda Hamlyn - Neapolitan/Tarantella; John Gilpin, Annette Chappell - Tirolese.
Center Bolero dancer: Joan McClelland with Eileen Ward (L) and Paula Hinton (R)
In the above photo B1 is correct, but changes were made in the other poses.
The front couple should be in a sideward *tombé* fall,
as performed by the front stage left couple in the picture below.

(Anthony Crickmay)

The Scottish Theatre Ballet.
Dancers (L to R): Elaine McDonald, Bruce Steivel, Amanda Olivier, Hilary Debden, Anne Allan (kneeling), Michael Beare, Sally Collard-Gentle, Harold King, Patricia Rianne.

APPENDIX

Notes on the Music

Printed Music

Soirées Musicales - Suite of Movements from Rossini - Arranged by Benjamin Britten is available from Boosey & Hawkes Ltd., 295 Regent Street, London W1.

Recorded Music

A suitable recording of the music is available on Cassette Tape under the Decca label, index number 425 659-4LM and priced £5.49.

www.ingramcontent.com/pod-product-compliance
Lightning Source LLC
Chambersburg PA
CBHW081116080526
44587CB00021B/3617